REMEMBERING DICK MILLER
by Terry Thome

Miller as Walter Paisley in HOLLYWOOD BLVD. (1976) Copyright New World Pictures.

When Dick Miller died on January 30, 2019, I found I was at a loss for the appropriate words to adequately describe the man. Indeed, as I'm writing these very words, I'm finding it difficult to describe just how important he was to a generation (or two! or three!) of exploitation film aficionados. It's not that his presence was neglected when he was alive. No, in fact he very much knew how highly regarded he was as a B-Movie legend. There have been books written, magazine articles by the ream, and a comprehensive film documentary that all adoringly explain why this man must command your attention.

Born on Christmas Day 1928 to an Opera singer and a printer in the Bronx, he was to become the consummate American character actor, making appearances in over 120 theatrical features and about 60 television appearances between 1955 and 2015 (that's 60 years, kids!). He began his career in entertainment as a writer for television in New York City but he eventually migrated to California to try his luck in Hollywood. He lived there for over a year, writing and selling science fiction stories before making his film debut in the Roger Corman cheapie, *Apache Woman*. Miller was dependable, affable, and (most importantly) available. He took part in most of Roger Corman's late 50s/ early 60s output, even taking the lead in *Rock All Night* and *A Bucket of Blood*, the latter giving him his most notable role as Walter Paisley; a character he revisited often over the next few decades.

When Roger Corman founded New World Pictures in 1970, it was only natural that Miller would be a substantial part of the in house productions. New World became an on-the-job film school and training ground for an entire generation of filmmakers including (but not limited to) Paul Bartel, Johnathan Kaplan, Lewis Teague, Barbara Peters, Johnathan Demme, Allan Arkush, and Joe Dante. It was with Dante that Dick Miller had his most high profile exposure. Miller was Dante's good luck charm and has been a featured player in every Joe Dante directed movie from *Hollywood Boulevard* (1976) to *Burying The Ex* (2014). He also showed up in Dante directed television shows, including *Amazing Stories* (1985) and *Police Squad!* (1982).

Throughout the 1980s and 1990s, Miller found steady work with bit parts in larger budgeted films as well as higher profile roles in more modest budgeted fantasy and horror films. Arguably, his most famous role was as Murray Futterman in Dante's anarchic horror comedy *Gremlins* (1985), a role he reprised in the sequel *Gremlins 2: The New Batch* (1991). It was *Gremlins* that gave him a new, younger generation of film goers whose parents were their age when he ate flowers as Burson Fouch in *Little Shop of Horrors* (1960).

In the new century, the 70-year-old Miller showed few signs of slowing down. Yet another generation of filmmakers began casting Miller in their films as a cultural touchstone. Even at his advanced age, Dick Miller never phoned it in. When he was hired to give a Dick Miller performance, he gave a Dick Miller performance, no punches pulled. That was his magic. Whatever film he appeared in, when he was on screen he gave the production something special that would never be replicated by another actor. He always took things to another level simply by being there.

In the last decade of his life, he still made the occasional film appearance but he devoted a substantial amount of his time showing up at conventions and film retrospectives. When he and his fans would meet, it was obvious that there was a little love affair happening. His fans adored him and he seemed to bask in it. In 2014, Elijah Drenner film biography *That Guy Dick Miller* premiered to raves at film festivals. Four years later, in 2018, Caelum Vatnsdal's essential tome *You Don't Know Me, But You Love Me: The Lives of Dick Miller* was released in hardback. It was the final word on a magnificent, if unlikely, career.

On December 27th, 2018, a Birthday bash was held in Burbank, CA for Dick Miller's 90 year on the planet. The place was filled with family,

HAPPY CLOUD MEDIA LLC PRESENTS:

EXPLOITATION NATION

DOWN THE RABBIT HOLE	2
REMEMBERING DICK MILLER	3
ON THE (PURGATORY) ROAD WITH MARK SAVAGE	6
SASH SPEAKS! AN INTERVIEW WITH MELINDA MCDOWELL	15
KUCHAR REVIEWS	22
THE DREAM LOGIC OF GABE BARTALOS	25
THE WISDOM & SYNCHRONICITY OF CARMINE CAPOBIANCO	38
PSYCHOS IN LOVE (1987)	43
HER NAME WAS CHRISTA, HIS NAME IS LONNIE: THE RETURN OF JAMES L. EDWARDS	45
ALL THE SECRETS OF THE LIGHT: AN INTERVIEW WITH FILMMAKER HENRIQUE COUTO	55
BRITAIN'S MORAL PANIC	68
THE CENSORSHIP OF SHATTER DEAD	74
THE FILMS OF SCOOTER McCRAE	80
DEVIL DOG: THE HOUND FROM HELL	84
I'D BUY THAT FOR A DOLLAR!	92
THE WIND AND THE LION (1975): THOUGHTS AND MUSINGS	97
THE PATRON SAINT OF THE UNCOOL: HOW REVEREND JEN MILLER'S ARTISTIC LEGACY KEPT NYC WEIRD	105

Exploitation Nation is published by Happy Cloud Media, LLC
Vol. 1, No. 7 © 2019

Amy Lynn Best:
Publisher
Mike Watt:
Editor
Carolyn Haushalter:
Asst. Editor
Ally Melling & Carol Melling:
Copy Editors
Ryan Hose:
Layout & Art Design

Contributors:
Dr. Rhonda Baughman
Justin Channell
Mike Haushalter
Jason Lane
Scooter McCrae
Ross Snyder
Terry Thome
Doug Waltz
Bill Watt

Cover art:
"Hell and High Water"
by Phillip R. Rogers

Logo created by:
Ryan Hose

All photographic and artistic content copyright the original holders and is included here for promotional purposes only. No rights are implicit or implied.

Exploitation Nation is published quarterly by Happy Cloud Media, LLC (Amy Lynn Best and Mike Watt, PO Box 260, Venetia, PA 15367). Exploitation Nation Issue #7 (ISBN 978-1-951036-16-4) is copyright 2019 by Happy Cloud Media LLC. All rights reserved. All featured articles and illustrations are copyright 2019 by their respective writers and artists. Reproductions of any material in whole or in part without its creator's written permission is strictly forbidden. Exploitation Nation accepts no responsibility for unsolicited manuscripts, DVDs, stills, art, or any other materials. Contributions are accepted on an invitational basis only.

Visit Us at Facebook.com/ExploitationNation

DOWN THE RABBIT HOLE

Once upon a time, the skies were black with indie filmmakers.

There were hundreds of us, it seemed, filling the dealer's rooms of every horror convention, our tables stacked with VHS and DVDs. We were distributed through Sub Rosa (headed by filmmaker Ron Bonk, The Vicious Sweet), and Tempe Entertainment (run by filmmaker JR Bookwalter, Ozone), and E.I. Entertainment (run by filmmaker Mike Raso, Ghoul School) and Troma Entertainment (run by filmmaker Lloyd Kaufman, Tromeo and Juliet).

We were members of various "waves," as defined by the late Andy Copp (The Mutilation Man—whose one-time blog gives our publication its name), arguably begun by Tim Ritter and his 35mm indie opus Truth or Dare, and Bookwalter's Super-8mm epic, The Dead Next Door. During the VHS boom and the rise of the mom-'n-pop video stores of the '80s, an indie could actually make a great deal of money as a filmmaker. We thought with the rise of DVD—those of us "Second Wavers," as per Andy, working in the DV format—the same would be true. But the DVD wave didn't last very long. Netflix and streaming video became the norm, putting to death the rental houses, large and small. Now the Blockbuster juggernaut has only one remaining store in operation in all of the U.S.

Amazon Prime seemed like it would pick up the slack and give Indies the outlet we'd all yearned for, but even that was short-lived. We watched as the pay-out "per view" dropped to a few pennies. Then there was the mysterious purge that eliminated whole libraries from the Prime catalog. No explanation was given, no appeal would be heard.

The cost of making a good movie didn't decrease, but the return did. Some of us took breaks from filmmaking. Life and family demanded that we find "real" careers in offices and retail. Bitterness increased, as did sadness. Eventually came acceptance. This is the world now. Indies aren't any more valued than we ever were. Don't cry for us, Argentina—pick up our movies!

The folks in this issue have been around forever. Many of us may have not made a movie in years, going-on decades, but like they say: Indie filmmakers never die; we just store ourselves in cool, dry places.

Until we fade away.

HAPPY CLOUD MEDIA

CELEBRATING 20 YEARS

friends, well-wishers and admirers. Dick wore his pink suit jacket, much to the dismay of his wife of 52 years, Lainie. There was reminiscing, laughter, music and dancing. The man of the hour was treated like the king he was. It was his final public appearance. 34 days later, he was gone. He died of natural causes.

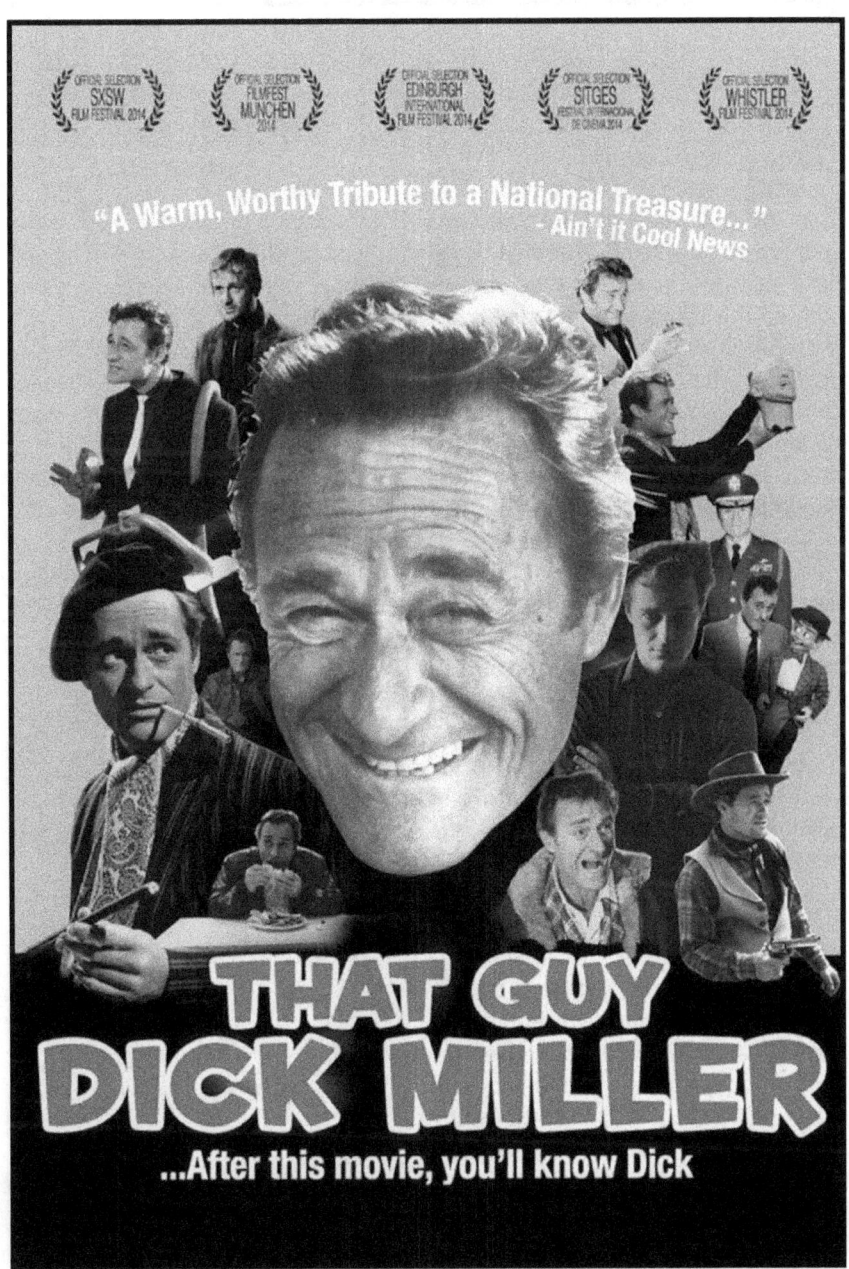

ON THE (PURGATORY) ROAD WITH **MARK SAVAGE**

You're driving down a winding country road. Off to the side is a dirty camper, covered with spray-painted messages offering salvation. "Absolution on Wheels," the camper declares. It's the quintessential confessional, American poverty-style. Whatever you do, don't confess to theft. There's a special place in Hell for thieves, and Father Vincent is all too willing to send you there.

Purgatory Road is the latest film from Australian expatriate Mark Savage, a neo-noir about religious fervor, guilt, death, and attrition. The off-road confessional contains a murder room overseen by two brothers: Father Vincent (Gary Cairns), who sets the fatal penance, and his brother, Michael (Luke Albright), who has to clean up afterwards.

As a child, Vincent confronted a thief robbing his home, but does nothing to stop her. The theft sets off a chain of events that leads to the family's ruin and sets Vincent on a path towards serving the church as he sees fit, bullying his younger brother into helping him send thieving sinners to God. But their squeaky machine is about to be greased by a new and chaotic element in the form of the unhinged Mary Francis (Trista Robinson), a helium-voiced killer in schoolgirl attire, about to bring the brothers' world crashing down around them.

"*Purgatory Road* grew out of a road trip," Savage tell me. "Things you see while driving down roads you've never been on. The idea of a closed confessional was always intriguing, and I liked the idea of a travelling confessional, with a priest inside, going from town to town. I saw this vehicle up ahead of us. I've

always been interested in the idea of confession. I did myself participate in confession when I was younger, as we were compelled to go to church. We were compelled to go to confession by my mother or by the school, and I'd say, 'Well, hold on, I don't know that I have anything to confess.' So I would even sometimes make something up. That felt like a sin in itself. I thought that was worse! And that then mingled with another concept I've been fascinated in, the idea of someone completely dedicated to a particular mission. That they become blind to whether the mission is good or bad for other people. To them it's just a mission they're on. And I think in a way, it's carried across to a lot of people—like suicide bombers, someone who is killing a hundred people for their allegiant, never thinking whether what they're doing is the right thing. Because I don't feel those people do think 'what I'm doing is terrible and I'm going to burn in Hell.' No, they think they're going to Heaven. I think those ideas are what informed the film, as well as my own thoughts about Catholicism, and it being mostly informed by good priests and bad priests that I've known when I was younger. Which is why the film does have a good priest. I didn't want it to be a complete attack on the church. I think it's good to have some balance. To me, the good priest [Father Joe, played by Geoff Falk] was a representative of the people who I've met who were good. There were some good priests in school, despite the fact that a quarter of them were beating kids up and the others were molesting them. Half of them were actually decent."

Teaser art for Purgatory Road.
All photos copyright and courtesy Mark Savage.

The primary motivation for both Vincent and Michael—and for Catholics the world over—is guilt. Vincent holds himself completely responsible for the collapse of his family, due to his inaction, allowing the thief to get away. Michael feels beholden to his brother, joining the mission to rid the world of other thieves, and the guilt starts to crush him. For Vincent, there is no other motivation. During confessions, he seems bored by the workaday sins of the rural confessors. Only the admission of theft gets his blood—and theirs—flowing. And, of course, Mary Francis is immune to guilt, which makes her presence in the brothers' lives that much more chaotic, bringing Michael's moral crisis into the forefront.

"Father Vincent doesn't really have a moral crisis," Savage explains, as Vincent feels he's on a mission for

God. "He starts to have one towards the end, but by then it's really too late for him. But that's when he starts panicking, after Mary Francis kills [a girl]. That's when he starts to feel the regret. Not sure if he's doing the right thing any longer. Also he's been severely compromised by her presence in his life, which is of course suggested by his interest in intimacy or sex. With the first woman that they kill and he can't stop staring at her panties while she's lying on the floor. You sort of know that he's quite vulnerable and quite susceptible to that kind of influence. And of course, Mary Francis provides that. And he just loses it then. I think Michael would have let it go on for a few more years. People do things like that. When they're in terrible situations, it takes a sense of crisis to get them out of it. Even the familiarity of the miserable is often still preferable to the challenge of making major changes. I think it gets to a point for Michael where everything is going in a very wrong direction. And he knows that she's become the main problem. There's the moment when Vincent says, 'I don't know if I can trust you, Brother.' And Michael says, 'I'm not the one you should be worried about.'"

Another exchange between the brothers reveals their mindset. When Vincent tells his brother that the path before them seems unclear. Michael responds, "Maybe if you stop killing people."

To which, Vincent replies, "Don't say anything you'll regret."

Michael's guilt is compounded when he inadvertently brings Mary Francis into their lives, realizing quickly that she's an unpredictable force. "Early on, [Michael] knows she's trouble despite the fact that he knows he's responsible for her surviving. He advises her to not mention stealing in the confessional. To me, that irony is that the guy that who is most compromised by her is also the one saved her ass from being decimated in the Confessional by Vincent. There was an earlier draft [in the script written by Savage and Tom Parnell] where Mary Francis *does* confess to theft. But in the film, she doesn't." Otherwise, she'd be cut to bits and in the ground with the rest of those Vincent "saved."

Those familiar with Savage's films know to expect violence. His films are often meditations on violence, and the effects violence has on the "average" person's psyche. Take, for instance, the completely unnecessary Hell brought upon his protagonist in *Defenseless*. Because she is unwilling to sign a simple contract, her loved ones are murdered, she's raped, bludgeoned, and thrown into the sea, only to be reborn later to enact bloody vengeance. The violence in *Defenseless* is impossibly real at times, and the sadism creates something even more terrible to behold. For Savage, violence serves a different purpose for each project. In *Marauders*, it's meant to thrill. In *Purgatory Road*, each act is tinged with regret and sadness.

"I approach each project thinking about how best to integrate violence. It's of course a cinematic trope. I think that's one of the chief reasons I was drawn to that kind of material. It's so cinematic depicting violence and action and non-verbal conflict. As the years go by and you make more films I've just tried to integrate all the elements that are there and will continue integrating to the point that there is relevancy with every element, rather than just elements present to only thrill. Those kinds of elements are noble in their own way. Certainly all of us all love films that are just [a collection] of elements thrown in for fun. I'm definitely drawn to stories where people's personalities are in conflict with themselves. I think that's a concept I'm interested in. Even going back to silly stuff I'd done. I think in a way we all are at war with ourselves. It's a constant thing. People say that even if you commit a crime and don't get caught, you really still are caught by yourself. Unless you're someone who has absolutely no conscience, but there really aren't many people like that. But most people don't really have a good relationship with the bad things they've done. Those tend to really permeate their consciousness until the day they die."

Violence in cinema is nothing new, and it's a subject many filmmakers enjoy exploring, despite the inevitable outcry it detracts. Violence in movies—like video games, comic books, and every form of, ironically, non-Biblical entertainment—is the root of all evil, of course. Our elected officials, our moral guides, all say this, so it must be true. "I think it really just comes from my own self-awareness of what I do and the struggle to do it. Even from a very young age, the films I was drawn to weren't necessary what other people were—I was often belittled for the types of films I made with regards to that kind of conflict. I definitely have a love-hate relationship with filmmaking. The business side is just so terrible. I've never been able to really find someone who could totally take care of the business side and let me take care of the creative side. I've had to do both. That's in a way given me that love-hate relationship with it. I've done a lot of films—obviously not as many as someone like Takashi Miike—my god, I look like a complete slacker compared to people like that. I think you're always pushing against the grain when you're, in loose terms, 'an artist'. When you pursue artistic things, you're almost always an outsider, and the outsider is an aspect of making films, and has often impacted me and made a lot more obvious the conflict within myself, in order to go 'Okay, you're doing this,' but also you're life's going up and down financially, it's going up and down creatively, and that never changes. Then my struggle is also sometimes, 'God, I should just do something much more stable.' I'm

Sensitive New Age Killer...sorry, HITMAN'S HERO - new art for the upcoming remastered release.

always in conflict with myself, 'you keep wanting to make these films but at the same time you're jeopardizing other things that maybe you need to focus on'. But at the same time the drive and need to tell the story, maybe in different forms, results in a sort of schizoid perspective on what you do in a larger sense. I kind of make a living at it, but at the same time, it's not something that gives me any great peace."

Savage's career started in his native Australia, first making short punk-attitude movies with his brother and friends. Little nasty jokes with violent punchlines, the kinds of things you do when you're a disaffected young artist. From these shorts grew the misanthropic film *Marauders*, starring Colin Savage and a magnificent mullet as the leader of a trio of vicious thugs whose violence triggers an equally violent response from their community. In the end, Coin, as "Emilio" manages to deny the mob its vengeance by taking his own life, mostly out of pure meanness. While *Marauders* has a very rough feel, Savage moved to more thoughtful stories, like the bleak *Defenseless* and the fun *Hitman's Hero* (aka *Sensitive New Age Killer*). But in the mid-2000s, Australia didn't have a lot to offer someone with designs on a career as a filmmaker, so Savage pulled up stakes and moved to the U.S. (Where we're known for embracing artists and supporting their dreams. He said, masking bitterness and irony.)

"I very much feel like an outsider all the time. My films almost always reflect outsider values and from an outsider perspective. I was an outsider in Australia, so I came here, and then here I still don't feel like I'm the kind of filmmaker making the kinds of things other people are making. Or that I'm even in a sort of club. There is like a film festival club here, where people are always getting into certain festivals, I'm not even in those clubs! I'm not sure where I fit in. I still feel an intense kind of drive, but I don't know if that's necessarily a good thing."

While Savage found a career as a cameraman in between his own projects, he came to learn that the challenges to making a film and getting it seen are never-ending. "Often the lead up feels like it's building to something that never comes. Now there are more films than ever. Even projects that have been announced – this film's being remade or this film's someone's bought the book and they're making this film— I've noticed that there's often more interest in the lead-up and when the film comes out you hardly even know it's out, it gets a couple of reviews, and then it dies. I even have people saying to me, 'I can't wait to see you're new film,' and I tell them, 'Well, look, it's already out. 'Looking forward to it'? It's already out. On Amazon, it's like two dollars, four dollars, or it's out on Blu-ray.' It's a weird thing—it comes out and then it just kind of fades. It's the equivalent of being out in the cinema for two or three years. So that kind of marketing myself, I had to remind myself, 'It's not just about marketing for three or four weeks. You almost have to have an adjusted marketing campaign every three months to remind people it exists."

Working as a camera operator on shows like *Big Brother* and TV pilots gave Savage the opportunity to tour most of the United States, getting to see our big melting pot as a series of different countries. The Heartland is as distinct from New England as it is the West Coast. But while wearing the filmmaking hat, Savage only saw potential locations. "In the last, say, three or four years, I was working for a company shooting TV pilots. So I reckon I traveled to twenty-five states doing those. Incredible locations here. It's definitely eye-opening. The film I made before *Purgatory* was *Stressed to Kill* [starring Bill Oberst and Amand Assante]. I'd done a pilot for a show set in Panama City, in Florida, and I love that area. And then I'd met Tom Parnell, with whom I'd worked on a couple of movies, and he was from Florida as well. And I thought that *Stressed to Kill* would really work in Florida, because of the heat and the overall oppressive feel of the weather does kind of, like, piss people off. Mississippi, where we shot *Purgatory Road*, came about thanks to people from the Mississippi film office being familiar with Chris Smirna, the line producer. They came and saw us in L.A. and said, 'Why don't you consider shooting in Mississippi?' They sent us a lot of marketing footage and stills. We had a look and we really liked it, but that was the main reason we shot in Mississippi. It was definitely cheaper than shooting in California, but then everywhere is cheaper than shooting in California. I haven't made much here. I made *Pond Scum* here in California, of course that's very low budget. That's the next one that's going to be released. That's something that was five or six years in the making, shooting when I could. It wasn't necessarily dependent on adhering to a schedule or a budget. I don't feel—it's not really viable shooting in California. It's too expensive here."

Pond Scum, one of the most

Trista Robinson as Mary Francis.

evocative titles for a film I've seen in some time, co-stars Renee and Ward Boult. The latter name may be familiar to longtime readers of *Femme Fatales* Magazine, which featured the photographer's stark and uncomfortable imagery. "*Pond Scum* is closer in a way to something like *Marauders*, it's a very nihilistic film. At the same time it was really very much a vehicle for Renee. She's had a really tough life, a lot negativity, a lot of abuse. I really like her. I think she's very talented. It [came about by] really just us talking, her and I collaborating on the story. Initially it's very much about the downward spiral her life takes due to her relationship with her son. The idea that she's a mother and she can't give her son what she wants to, and she starts to question then why her son should live. It's very dark and a pretty brutal film. I'm a big admirer of the Japanese director, Kōji Wakamatsu. One film of his in particular, *The Man Who Assaulted 13 People*, was so fucking brutal and unrepentantly ugly and not caring how ugly it was. It was very ferocious in its pacing and subject matter—I thought with [*Pond Scum*], 'I don't care if anyone likes this film, I just want to make it.' It wasn't made with any sense of the audience; it doesn't have to make money because it was completely self-financed. I don't really care if it gets embraced or despised. I just want to get it out there."

Locations are important for nearly every film, but for Savage, terrain is almost an additional character. The area is important to the development of character. Place has a lot to do with persona. "I used to be quite paranoid while hiking. Even hiking in a place like Death Valley, I'm looking up at those hills wondering, is someone looking back at me? Someone who looks like Michael Berryman is up there in those hills. Of course, the other part of me goes, 'Come on, nobody is going to be able

Michael Lebeau as Young Vincent.

to survive in this kind of heat for years on end.' I think it is really important to get away from that place in my head. I even have a couple of projects aimed at younger audiences. I've got a soccer film that I'm trying to get financed at the moment. It's almost like a *Field of Dreams*, with soccer and kids. That kind of style. I don't feel separated from that kind of material. To me, everything is about human behavior. Sometimes the genre is like the picture frame, but the picture is always human behavior. It's still about desires, and what someone wants, and what someone else wants to stop them from getting. That, to me, if it hasn't got that, I'm not interested. If it isn't exploring the inconsistency of human beings.

"That is what matters. It's always important to me to explore what a person is about, what their wounds are. Wounds are always interesting. Everybody has wounds. Finding how your behavior is impacted by the wounds that you have. That's everything to me. Every script that I write, and even other scripts that I read, that's the question I always have [for the writer], 'what's happened to them, what harm has been done to them that's impacted the way that they feel and the way that they think, and the way that they behave in a dysfunctional way. It's all the wounds."

A question rarely asked filmmakers who truck in violent themes is what they do to recover from the grim fantasy. How do you rid the cinematic violence from your own life? "I suppose that when making these kinds of films, particularly *Marauders*, *Defenseless* and *Pond Scum*, I think I recover the way a lot of people do. I just try to make sure I'm doing other things in my life, which I didn't making *Marauders*. I do other things like going hiking, taking photos, watching Studio Ghibli films, which helps a lot. I find that they help you get to a really good place. Watching a film like *Totoro* or *Spirited Away*, I really love those films. I could totally make something like that! I don't look things like that and say, 'No, that isn't me.' In my films I really try to counter the ugliness with beauty. I always feel the desire to do that, with stark contrast. I try to live a life that's a very stark contrast to the movies I make. That's why I have no desire to live in inner city 'cool' film areas. Those places are usually very busy and chaotic, and I don't enjoy living in places like that. I've already got that place in my head. I used to live in West Hollywood, which is often considered the kind of hub of the film business, but I hated living there. It's just so noisy, everyone is in your face all the time. Every person you'd meet had a script or wanted to talk to you about something. I much preferred to live in a much quieter place where you can get your thoughts and head back together again. Listen to music, go on hikes, that sort of thing. I couldn't stand living where those kinds of films come from."

Purgatory Road is enjoying a run on Amazon's streaming platform. Interested viewers should head there now (and then check out *Stressed to Kill* while you're at it. "*Purgatory Road* is probably the first film I've done where I pretty much feel good about everything. Every other film I have that feeling where 'God, I wish I'd done that differently, or I wish I hadn't done that, or I wish I had more time for that, or that was really bad writing, I wish I'd explained that more, or explained that less.' This first time I don't feel much like that. It's pretty much what I wanted it to be. I don't wake up in the middle of the night thinking, 'Fuck!' I used to do that. I do still think like that occasionally. 'I wish I could get every copy on every platform and take out that scene!' Of course you can't do that, it's ridiculous. And of course it's never over. You're always attached to them. They're like children—when your kid turns 18, that doesn't mean it's the end. You know? It's just the beginning of a different stage."

Renae Boult in the upcoming, fun for the whole family POND SCUM.

SASH SPEAKS! AN INTERVIEW WITH MELINDA MCDOWELL
by Ross Snyder

In the decade that bred some of the most audacious and groundbreaking midnight films in the annals of American history (including John Waters' *Pink Flamingos*, David Lynch's *Eraserhead*, and Gerard Damiano's *Deep Throat*), few could rightfully hold a candle to the mix of jaw-dropping lunacy, uninhibited carnality, and touching sentimentality on display in Curt McDowell's brilliant 1975 cult epic *Thundercrack!*.

Shot on 16mm, black & white film and clocking in at an astounding 150+ minute running time, *Thundercrack!* was best described by a local San Francisco journalist in its day as "a raunchy, campy epic modeled on early Warhol efforts, those outrageous films starring Divine, the most static passages of *Night of the Living Dead*, and some of James Whale's *The Old Dark House*, with a little Tennessee Williams thrown in for leavening."[1] As if that concoction wasn't enough to melt the mind of even the most adventurous moviegoer, *Thundercrack!* also contained non-simulated, XXX hardcore sex scenes of both the straight and gay variety, the awkward cocktail of which led to a well-documented history of divided audiences and distribution woes.

It was largely the brainchild of two notorious underground raconteurs whose chance meeting at the San Francisco Art Institute (as teacher and student) lead to a fruitful partnership that would eventually spawn *Thundercrack!* from its loins. The Indiana-born director Curt McDowell, who made his way West to study painting at the Art Institute, would come to amass a stunning cache of candidly autobiographical and joyously salacious short films before unleashing the porn-chic meets avant-garde, XXX opus *Lunch* on audiences in 1972.

Although based on a story idea by himself and collaborator Mark Ellinger, Curt would wisely entrust the screenplay of his feature film follow-up *Thundercrack!* to his teacher, mentor, and partner George Kuchar, who along with his twin brother Mike, was one of the key figures of the New York underground movie scene of the 1960's. With his low-fi, DIY aesthetics and penchant for cut rate, 1950's Sirk-esque melodramas made during the height of Warhol inspired minimalism, George set himself apart from his contemporaries and

---

1 H. Fairbanks (1976) NewsWest, April 30-May 14

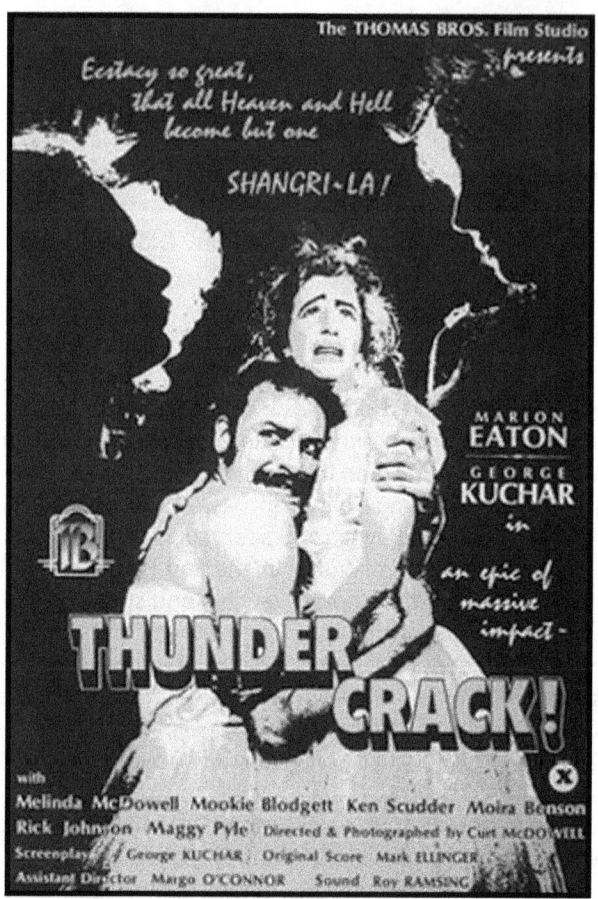

would eventually cement his place as one of the most influential and important underground filmmakers in the history of American cinema. It was precisely the duality of Curt's gleeful and celebratory attitude contrasting with George's guilt ridden and paranoia-laced views towards the subject of sex that makes *Thundercrack!* such an anomalous cinematic journey to partake in.

In the midst of all the humping and assorted transgressions, several pivotal and unforgettable performances (in addition to Mark Ellinger's remarkable piano score) elevate *Thundercrack!* far beyond the heights of its filmic counterparts. The brilliant Marion Eaton as the lonesome and sorrowful Mrs. Gert Hammond whose isolated Prairie Blossom estate is suddenly ambushed by a cavalcade of unusual travelers seeking shelter from a storm. George Kuchar himself as the disturbed circus employee Bing, who's tormented by a secret lust for his escaped pet gorilla Medusa. And most importantly, lest we forget the dazzling Melinda McDowell as Sash, Roo's notoriously red-assed riding companion from Tucson who ultimately devotes herself to

Chandler and his fervent desire to burn the House of Phillips Unlimited girdle factory to the ground. As Curt's beloved sister and muse, the doe-eyed Melinda became a fearless collaborator in Curt's prurient film oeuvre after following him to California and devoting herself freely to his film related exploits. She would go on to star in the lead role of Curt's extraordinary, autobiographical, 1985 masterpiece *Sparkle's Tavern*, as well as small roles in films by both the Kuchar Brothers and Barbara Linkevitch. Melinda continued to carry the artistic torch for her brother Curt following his AIDS related death in 1987, by archiving, restoring, and exhibiting his films, writings, and artworks for a whole new generation of fans to discover. I was delighted (as always) to sit down with my longtime friend Melinda McDowell to discuss her life in film as well as her brother Curt's indelible and gooey mark on the history of cinema.

Ross Snyder: What was life like for you and Curt growing up together in Indiana?

Melinda McDowell: Enviable! Not because we were well off financially, quite the opposite. But because we had parents and a sister who loved us unconditionally, always. We were supplied with everything we could want or need. I'd say a rich life for some not so rich folks! Curt loved us all but at some point, he needed to make his way out of Lafayette, Indiana. While still in high school he decided he'd like to hitchhike around Europe. He did, and our school let him return two years later to graduate! Art school was next on his mind.

RS: Curt eventually made his way to the Art Institute of San Francisco where he met and became the first student of the legendary underground filmmaker George Kuchar. George and Curt formed a fruitful relationship that would spawn many unforgettable film projects. Can you tell us a bit about Curt and George's collaborative process together?

MM: [Laughs] George and Curt, such a perfect combination. I recall when Curt had given George the premise for *Thundercrack!* and asked if he would write the screenplay. Upon reading George's 92-page handwritten script he was laughing so hard. "George! I never said anything about a gorilla or the circus!" Of course, it was left in. They were both incredibly kind and were receptive to each other's creative ideas. I'm so grateful for the years they spent together, being in each other's films, creating priceless entertainment that we're still loving today. I believe my favorite just might be *Wieners and Buns Musical*. It's a crowd pleaser for sure.

RS: You ended up co-starring opposite George in Curt's film *Beaver Fever*. When did Curt entice you to move out to San Francisco and get involved with his filmmaking endeavors? Did you always have an ambition to become an actress?

MM: I had no thoughts at all of being an actress and *Beaver Fever* only happened because Curt and George stopped to visit our family in Indiana while on their way to New York to visit George's friends and family. Curt suggested doing a film there in Lafayette and of course we did. Upon their return to San Francisco, Curt called to tell me he needed a few more shots for the film and that I should come on out. A thinly veiled and successful ruse to extricate me from the Midwest. I left my job, my boyfriend, said my farewells to Mom and Dad, and drove to San Francisco. Even after 43 years had passed, I think Mom was still hopeful I'd return to Indiana to live someday.

RS: What was San Francisco like in that era of the 1970s?

MM: Oh my! If you were to ask any of us who were the right age in that particular decade, I believe the universal response is a glassy-eyed, cheesy-grinning face, mumbling, "Ahh...." And San Francisco was the perfect place to be. Overflowing with culture, creativity, and definitely all the sex, drugs, and rock n' roll that anyone could handle. No consequences! There will not be a decade like that one again, ever.

RS: You also co-starred in George Kuchar's remarkable 1975 underground cult feature, *The Devil's Cleavage*. Do you have any amusing recollections from that shoot or working with George as a director?

MM: Oh dear. Co-starred? Ha! My appearance onscreen was so brief that I actually forgot that I was in that one. I attended a screening of it and was shocked when I saw my name in the titles. That tiny, embarrassing scene for *The Devil's Cleavage* was filmed in my room at our house in Indiana at the same time as the *Beaver Fever* footage. I had just met George,

so I didn't feel like I could question his idea for that scene. George was always a delight, no matter if it was while directing, co-starring, or just visiting at home. We were always laughing.

RS: I know Curt was already well known to underground cineastes for his dazzling short works (as well as the feature-length, 1972 experimental XXX film *Lunch*). It seems like the timing was perfect for him to tackle an audacious and large-scale feature project such as *Thundercrack!*. When did you first hear about the project and what were your thoughts after reading George's astonishing completed screenplay?

Melinda with author Ross Snyder. Copyright and Courtesy...Ross.

MM: Yes, it was time for *Thundercrack!*, which was precisely the reason *Lunch* was made first. Curt and Mark Ellinger had come up with the idea for *Thundercrack!* but needed funding for such an undertaking. They decided to create *Lunch* first, hoping to amass enough income from it to fund the film they really wanted to do. It did help but it was the Thomas Brothers Film Studio that was able to cover the additional cost. George's screenplay was a wealth of comedy. We all were reading it together through tears of laughter. However, if Curt had filmed the entire screenplay, the film would've been four hours long. So, with reluctance, it had to be cut down.

RS: Aside from having little acting experience in front of the camera, you also had to perform real sex acts for the first time on film. Were you nervous to be cast by your brother in the role of Sash in *Thundercrack!*?

MM: I'm rarely nervous about things, this being no exception. I trusted Curt completely. So, when he asked me to be in this film I didn't hesitate. That carried through to all the films he asked me to do. No second thoughts ever. Definitely a new experience to be surrounded on all sides by a crew while doing those scenes. So, I might say I'm "adaptable."

RS: I know the film was shot in ten days at producer Charles Thomas' house which doubles as the Prairie Blossom farmhouse. Any funny stories you can recall from the set?

MM: I do recall the cast and crew running out the front door while gasping for air the moment the jars containing the pickled Mr. Hammond

were opened at the end of those ten days. They contained actual entrails in water and to say the stench was unbearable is understating it a bit. I've shared the story before about the peeled cucumber that Gert throws in the fruit bowl…but it's a good one! The character of Willene (Maggie Pyle) after saying, 'This looks refreshing!' takes a bite, but she was the only person in the cast and crew who didn't know that it was the actual cucumber that had been "utilized" earlier by Gert (Marion Eaton). Though a somewhat cruel prank, the consensus was that she deserved it for showing up onset drunk day after day and causing trouble for Curt.

RS: Once completed, the film's original 150-minute version had a successful sold out screening at New York's Anthology Film Archives as well as a rather infamous midnight screening at L.A.'s FILMEX. What are your memories from those two screenings?

MM: The New York audience was so appreciative, and AFA screened *Thundercrack!* once more a week later and it sold out again! Los Angeles was quite a different story. I do recall meeting Buck Henry, who had fought for the film to be in FILMEX by threatening to step down as a judge if it wasn't included. During the film's intermission two "firsts" happened. One was while I was in line for the restroom. Ladies were whispering and pointing at me, having just seen me onscreen moments before. Recognition of the dubious sort! The second thing was a mass exodus by horrified audience members who had gone into this screening blindly and were seeing things they surely were not prepared to see. Because this film has "a little something for everybody" is precisely the reason that it is not for everybody.

RS: *Thundercrack!* was notorious for audience walkouts and distribution setbacks in its day. It seemed to have had a very hard time finding its initial audience. Too salacious for the arthouse crowd. Too much chatter for the raincoat crowd. In more recent years, the film has become a beloved treasure to both cult, queer, avant-garde, and even horror film enthusiasts alike. Do you think it was simply ahead of its time? Do you think Curt would be pleased with the status the film holds with fans today?

MM: In thinking about it being "ahead of its time," I wonder exactly where *Thundercrack!* would fall into place as its right time. Does it have one? Maybe someone in the future will declare it to be "timely." I'm certain that Curt would not only be moved to tears at the love that is shown to this film so many decades later, but he'd be astonished that AMPAS would seek out all his films to restore and preserve in their vaults. He'd think there had been a mistake!

RS: I consider Curt's follow up feature *Sparkle's Tavern* to be his true masterpiece. With you, his muse cast in the titular role of Sparkle, it certainly seems like his most personal and autobiographical film in many respects. With it taking nearly a decade to reach completion, can you talk a bit about the making of the film and its arduous journey to the screen?

MM: *Sparkle's Tavern* has only recently been seen by more audiences, and it's nice to hear those kind words. The filming didn't take very long at all and our cast and crew had great fun with it. The complete set was built within one empty space; a loft above an auto repair / parking garage in the Tenderloin district of San Francisco. That significant gap in time between filming in '76 and completion in '84 was only because Curt ran out of funds until he received an N.E.A. grant for the project. Again, being boastful although Curt would not, I don't think he would've imagined *Sparkle's Tavern* receiving accolades decades later in the form of a 2014 National Film Preservation Foundation federal grant. Curt, still being honored long after he's gone.

RS: In 2016, I was lucky enough to see you host theatrical screenings of both *Thundercrack!* and *Sparkle's*

Tavern in addition to restorations of some of Curt's rarer works like *Taboo: The Single and the LP* & *Wieners and Buns Musical* (as part of the *Loads Of McDowell* retrospective at AFA). I know other retrospective screenings have taken place across the country. Are there any more upcoming plans for releasing or exhibiting Curt's work in the near future?

MM: The newly restored films have been seeing more and more screen time. We did have an evening of Curt's short films here in San Francisco recently thanks to Canyon Cinema. It's such a joy to see them with an audience. Especially when they are longtime fans of his work and are seeing one of the films for the first time. Many had not seen *The Mean Brothers Get Stood Up* or *Beaver Fever*, and seemed to appreciate them both. My job as caretaker of all Curt's films and artwork doesn't seem to be slowing down at all and I couldn't be happier about that. Curt lives on!

KUCHAR REVIEWS

SINS OF THE FLESHAPOIDS (1966)
Directed by Mike Kuchar
Starring Bob Cowan, George Kuchar and Donna Kerness
43 Minutes
Reviewed by Doug Waltz

A million years in the future after a nuclear apocalypse has devastated the human population, life continues on. The remainder of humanity have become a decadent race only interested in their most primal desires. Their every whim is catered by an indestructible race of androids known as the Fleshapoids, because of their realistic flesh like covering.

Xar (Bob Cowan) has become aware and tires of his owner (Gina Zuckerman). She threatens to pour water on him to make him rust so he kills her with a single blow. Then he makes his way to the castle of Prince Gianbeno (George Kuchar), who has Xar's true love Melenka (Maren Thomas) held as his fleshapoid slave. Meanwhile Princess Vivianna (Donna Kerness) is having an affair with Ernie (Julius Middleman) in the tower of their futuristic castle.

The Princess soon realizes that her Prince no longer cares for her and decides to escape with her beloved Ernie. During her escape she drops all of her riches she is taking with them and Ernie stops to collect them all. She realizes that Ernie is there for the money so she stabs him in the back and then kills herself.

Meanwhile, Prince Gianbeno finds Xar and Melenka making electrical love so he shuts down Melenka. Xar knocks him to the ground and reactivates Melenka. They use their electrical powers to destroy the Prince.

But then something bizarre occurs when Melenka falls to the floor thrashing about until she gives birth to a child, a little wind up robot.

In the end the fleshapoids find the love and reproduction that has been denied the doomed remnants of the human race.

The Kuchar Brothers were a part of the underground movie scene primarily in New York alongside others like Andy Warhol and Kenneth Anger. It would eventually mutate into the Cinema of Transgression and No Wave Cinema with people like Nick Zedd and Richard Kern.

Fleshapoids is one of their longer films, with a runtime of 43 minutes. There is no spoken dialogue. The soundtrack is a bombastic mishmash of public domain tracks and when people do speak their words appear as word balloons on the screen. A narrator (also Bob Cowan) fills in a few points of story along the way.

The people in the film dress like they are in Rome during the fall. A simple Brooklyn apartment is transformed into a castle with the use of draping silks and bizarre wall paintings. By conveniently referring to the androids as "fleshapoids," the Kuchar Brothers avoid any serious make up, with the exception of a little face paint on Xar, and a device (that looks like it was put on with electrical tape) on one of Melenka's breasts (when Prince Gianbeno shuts her down during the climax of the film).

The deep rich colors of the film gives it an Andy Milligan film feel, without all the angry shouting. The one exterior is a painting of a castle that also looks like a rocketship. During the electrical execution of the prince it goes back out to the painting where they have rigged one of the windows to flicker as he dies. Reminiscent of an animated *Monty Python* scene, it made the painting feel more real in the process.

The final aspect of the film is the message that we are all doomed. That things we make are better suited to our life than we are.

THE CRAVEN SLUCK (1967)
Written & Directed by Mike Kuchar
Starring Floraine Connors, Bob Cowan, George Kuchar
15 Minutes
Reviewed by Doug Waltz

Adele (Floraine Connors) is a bored housewife who decides to kill herself when her husband, Brunswick (Bob Cowan), leaves for work. He forgets his fountain pen and upon returning stops her from drowning herself, and then sends her out to walk the dog, Bocko (Played by Bocko the dog). It's then she runs into Morton

(George Kuchar) and the two share a moment that is glossed over when Kuchar's camera decides to film Bocko taking a shit instead. We discover that Morton is also married to the drug-addled Florence (Bob Cowan again). At no time do they try to hide that Bob is actually a man in bad drag but they play it straight. Later Morton is out and about and spies the lovely Marilyn Marmoset (Donna Kerness), who returns to her apartment. She strips down to her undergarments and spies Morton outside. She walks over to the door and unlocks it and walks back out of camera. The scene is just implied, but is probably one of the more powerful scenes in the film.

The next day Morton calls Adele to cancel their meet up for the day. Florence grabs the phone and tells Adele to leave her husband alone. Then flying saucers appear over Brooklyn and they disintegrate Adele. The black and white photography gives a New York from the '60s that you don't see many places in film. It is stark and washed out, much like Adele who believes that she is still desirable, but we can see that she is chipping away at the edges and desperate for any form of affection from anyone.

The opening credits are spoken by the narrator (Bob Cowan, again) who even spells the word 'marmoset' for us and explains that it's like the monkey with the same name.

The end is abrupt and can throw you off guard. The saucers are an obvious homage to Ed Wood's *Plan 9 From Outer Space*, but instead of props Kuchar uses lights and makes them more effective in the process regardless of how ludicrous their insertion into the narrative actually is.

I watched this as a warm up for *Sins of the Fleshapoids* and I think it captures the underground flavor of the Kuchar Brothers perfectly.

The legendary Brothers Kuchar: Mike and George.
Copyright unknown. All Rights Reserved.

THE DREAM LOGIC OF GABE BARTALOS

I'm just going to come out and say this: You've never seen a movie like *Saint Bernard*. It is unique unto itself and possibly the purest distillation of a "personal film" as you're likely to find. It was born from the mind of effects artist and filmmaker Gabe Bartalos.

He describes the plot as this: "'[A] musical composer hits an arc in his life that takes him down the rabbit hole as he mentally disintegrates.' I thought it'd be cool to explore a composer's descent into madness and how to visualize that. I decided that if it's going to be through dreams, I'd like to take this episodic [structure] that will lend itself to the narrative. And then I imagined scenarios that would lead to it. There are a lot of layers and density to *Saint Bernard*. As the film goes on, the Bernard character is slipping further and further from reality."

We meet the adult Bernard (Jason Dugre) as his mind has already begun deteriorating. Wandering along a freeway, he discovers the severed head and spinal cord of an enormous St. Bernard, and the bloody talisman becomes his companion during his journey into the abyss, a constant rotting reminder of his fragmenting reality. Because the film is entirely from Bernard's point of view, the audience has no frame of reference for the insane situations he finds himself in. There is no ground beneath our feet because Bernard is not grounded.

Anything even remotely benevolent becomes twisted and misshapen. A visit to Father Steele (the legendary trickster, Bob Zmuda) quickly becomes a nightmare of avarice; Miss Roadkill (Katy Sullivan) offers no assistance and he is forced to escape her by leaping into a pool of diarrhea spewed by "Static Boy"; the monstrous, trollish police are no help, not even after he fights his way through a hallway lined

The one and only STATIC BOY! (All photos courtesy and copyright Gabriel Bartalos)

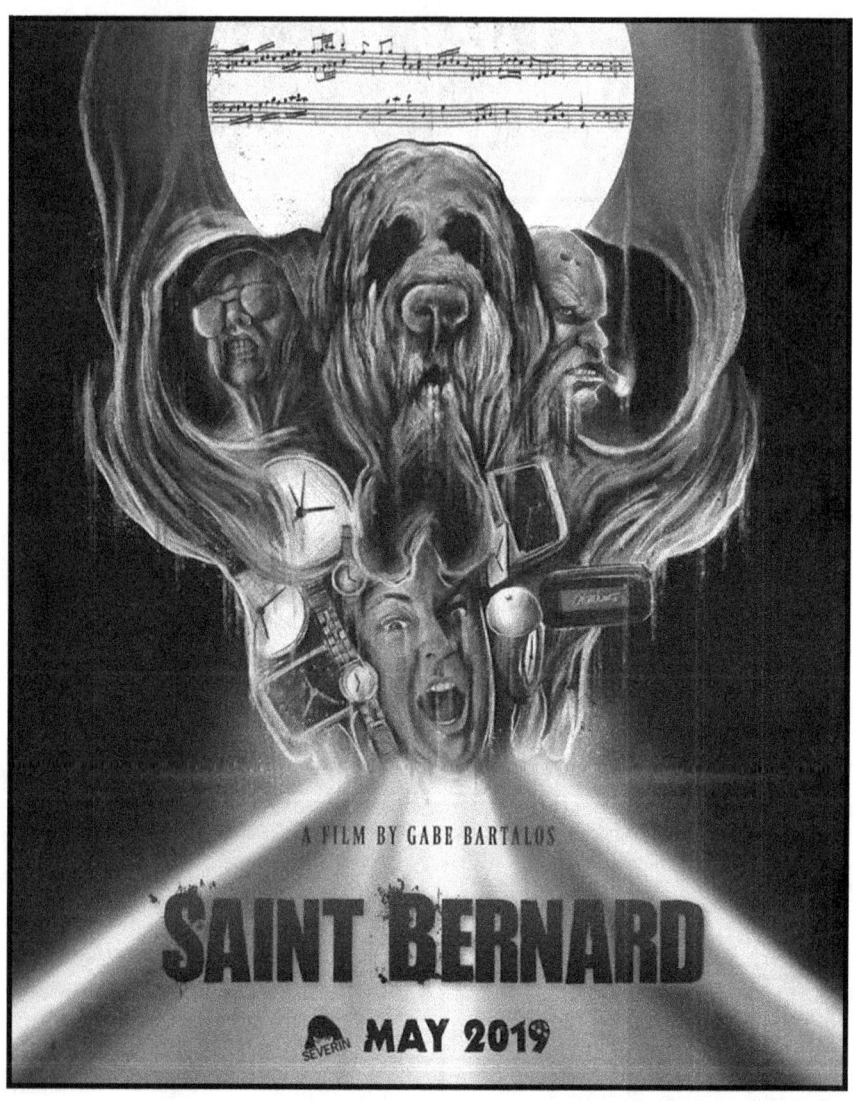

knee-deep with wine bottles; only Othello (Warwick Davis) provides any guidance—but none of these characters can be proven "real," not by Bernard and not by the audience. There is no escape for any of us.

"I'm a huge fan of dreams," says Bartalos. "I've recorded my dreams for a long time. I've always been fascinated by the spell that dreams have. Even when they dissolve when you wake up, that almost leads to the melancholy and the haunt of it. I thought that, since Bernard is deteriorating mentally and there's obviously decay of his brain, he's going to be confusing realities, almost like a fever dream, shifting in and out of what he perceives as real. So, dream logic was the perfect place to explore. I love in dreams, there are these little episodic mini-movies, little scenes, and at the time they seem unrelated, but, somehow, there's always a little thread or a mood or a character, something that overarches and connects them all.

"I looked at this very seriously in linking together the odyssey that Bernard goes on. I really tried to get that spell of what a dream is like. That was a choice I made to try and visualize for the viewing audience what his personal insanity might be like. We've all seen insanity and dreams portrayed in film, sometimes really effectively and sometimes not. I wanted to strip all that away and kind of really, through my own point of view, look at it almost surgically and see what I really have to do and how to write the script and shoot those scenes to really get that mood, which would be my form of storytelling to overall bundle this poor guy who's taken a bad trip."

As the nightmare unspools, Bartalos constantly yanks the rug out from under the viewer. "I think it's important for things to not always be fully explained. Even in a dream that's quite linear, there are always curveballs," he says. Just when we're convinced we're witnessing a hallucination, someone outside of Bernard's perspective witnesses something bizarre and reacts to it. So, whose hallucination is it, anyway?

He explains: "And you're like, 'Wait a minute—if this is Bernard's hallucination, why is this citizen witnessing this and reacting to it?' There were a few of those things that I put in there to add another layer of dream confusion. To ask, 'What is a dream?' Are we just witness to his hallucination? Not necessarily. Maybe that guy doesn't exist and we're witnessing a layer amongst a layer of visualization."

To give the impression that Bernard is both present and absent, literally slipping away from reality, Bartalos employed a variety of subliminal techniques. In one sequence, for example, Bernard wears a two-dimensional mask of his own face. In another:

"When he meets the Chief [played by Peter Iasillo Jr.], he walks into that bottle room. There's a series of shots where there is a woman projected on the wall, and she says 'Follow me,' and it cuts to a wide shot of the hallway. It's a mirror-vision. We shot the two of them walking and gesturing, and repeated and repeated; then, I projected onto them their exact movements, so that she was basically

The grotesque Chief of Police.

miming—she did a count, *one-two--three-wave-come on*—and he would walk in. So, in a sense, it's like a video shadow. But he doesn't appear in the video shadow. In the replay of the video shadow, I consciously left him out of it. She has a video shadow, he doesn't.

"Again, I was trying to figure out, how do I show him slipping out of his reality—out of his movie? He's vanishing, his soul is evaporating. Another example of pulling his character out of this reality is at the very end, when he's fighting with Uncle Ed [Jack Doroshow], he again—very quickly—is wearing a two-dimensional mask in a scream pattern. It's really cool. The audio design is so rich and dense, with the yelling and screaming, plunging into the water, the scream goes over the still photo of his face and you don't even catch it."

Saint Bernard comes closer to the pure depiction of a dream than virtually any other film I can think of, save perhaps Louis Malle's *Black Moon* (1975). It replicates dream logic so well that oftentimes, while watching, you may find your familiar surroundings disorienting.

"When I'm in a dream, sometimes they are extremely real," says Bartalos. "I don't know the science behind this, but my synapses have connected just like a real-life experience. Let's say I'm going through a tunnel that's closing in on me, and it's so real in the dream, just like it's in real life. Now, thinking back on it, there's no real emotional difference to me whether it was a dream or not. I would love to see the science on that. Are the same types of bridges, the same types of neural synapses fused when a dream experience is as impactful as a real-life one to my memory banks? Sometimes, it certainly feels exactly the same."

Personally, I've often wondered if film language has influenced our subconscious to the point where our brains present dreams like movies. Speaking for myself, I dream in cuts. Other filmmakers I know dream in both black-and-white and vivid Technicolor. Did our dreams change as our knowledge of film language grew? Going by that hypothesis, *Saint Bernard* is itself a dream.

"I was trying many different techniques to better learn the language of film and try to communicate to the audience in a very sublime, subliminal level his deterioration, his removal from reality," says Bartalos. "Someone who is immersed in cinema, does your dream reality follow what you like and surround yourself with? You'd have to take a poll. Wouldn't it be funny if arc welders, at the end of their dreams, experienced a bright white flash?"

True surrealism requires discipline. How often have we watched a filmic dream sequence fall flat on its face? Dreams are not literal—they cannot be. Nor can they be feature-length adventures that terminate with the dreamer waking up surrounded by loved ones.

Says Bartalos: "With surrealism, some people erroneously pass it off cynically as 'Aw, just throw a fish through the frame and you've got surrealism.' I think it's the opposite. When you're creating another world, you have to really know and own the project. I knew the narrative and how

I hoped to achieve the specific vibe of *Saint Bernard* inside and out, so every decision I made had to support every visual. Everything had to carry the other.

"When you move into surrealism, heavy symbolism, and metaphors, the real pleasure for me was to intellectually be totally aware of what I was doing and why. So, even when it seems nonsensical, it's not. It had a parallel in some sort or another for me that's informing and advising the trajectory of the film. I love that. I love that growth as a filmmaker, from thinking about and figuring out that process. Cerebrally, that's exciting. You have to be pretty careful with what you pick and choose so that you don't devalue the imagination that's been built up."

Bartalos's background is in special makeup effects. He made his debut on the bizarre catastrophe *Spookies* (1986) before moving on to a successful collaboration with Frank Henenlotter (who has a quick cameo in *Saint Bernard*), working on *Frankenhooker*, *Brain Damage*, the *Basket Case* sequels, and *Bad Biology*. Later work includes *Gremlins 2* and the *Leprechaun* series.

And anyone familiar with Bartalos's directorial debut, *Skinned Deep*, knows that Bartalos's visuals guide the story. Ostensibly a "killer mutant family" movie, with Dugre sporting a giant bulbous brain (the feature that gives his character his name), Warwick Davis as a philosophical maniac (named "Plates") with a penchant for crockery, a headless bodybuilder named "Creator" (played, appropriately, by an actor named "Headless Sean"), and the trap-mouthed "Surgeon General,"

Both Kurt Carley and Aaron Sims played the trap-jawed Surgeon General in SKINNED DEEP.

all battling a group of senior citizen bikers, *Skinned Deep* takes numerous sharp left turns, from a narrative standpoint, but is all wrapped in a dense production design that defines the film's reality.

Saint Bernard eschews any box you'd try to force it into. It's not really horror, though horrific things continue to happen. And while it's often funny, it's not a comedy. The locations are recognizable as existing in reality, but they're often off-kilter and menacing. There's no comfort to be found in *Saint Bernard*.

According to Bartalos, "When I knew I wanted it to celebrate a visual palate, I said, 'Boy, this is going to be fun. I'm going to enjoy this labor of love and play to my strengths.' I've always felt with creature design—even when we do a modest film—I've always wanted to push my designs. I feel like anyone can compete with

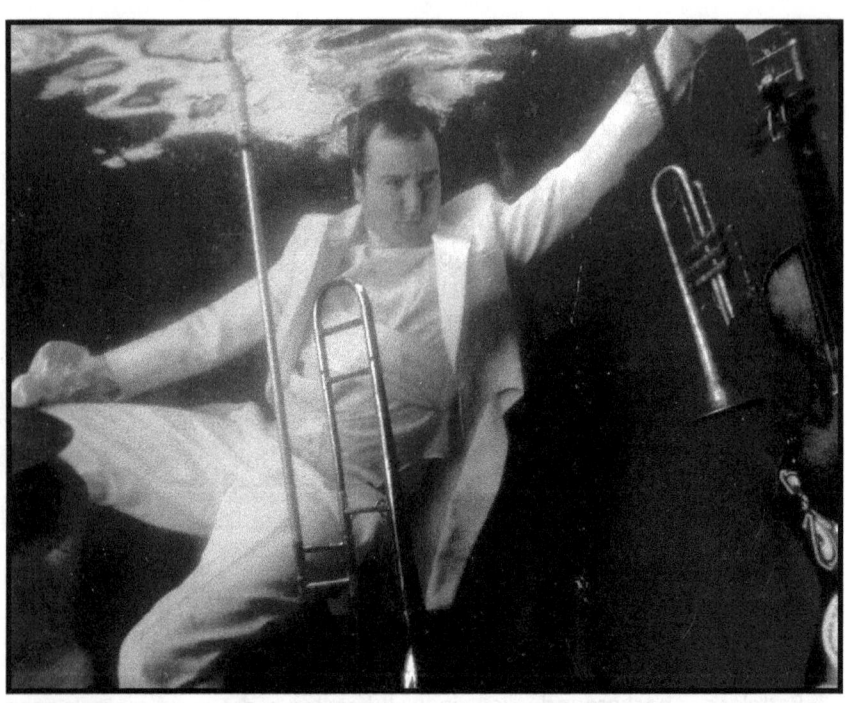

Jason Dugre as Bernard in SAINT BERNARD.

a major studio, or with dollar signs, with creativity. I think *Saint Bernard*'s a good example of just dreaming up things that people haven't seen before. It's easy enough to do if you have some time. It's showing off too.

"That density is something I'm attracted to. It helps amplify to an absurdist level the point I'm trying to make. So, specifically the police station, I figured there's no better way to introduce the Bernard character to the ineptitude he's about to face than through getting stuck in the 'system.' The minute you've got to deal with the DMV or the courts, say goodbye to your time! It's the precursor—you're going down this hallway, and the thousands of wine bottles let you know you're heading into the chief's domain. That's the hive. That's where they all come from, and it just gets weirder from there."

From a filmmaker standpoint, so much of the film as it unfolds prompts the question: "How did he pull that off?" How did Bartalos pull off a POV sequence of sky-diving uncooked chickens? How were the underwater sequences pulled off? Or the gag with an actor crashing through the window? Were all the wine bottles donated, or did Bartalos sacrifice his liver for the cause? Every sequence has multiple layers, visually and emotionally—the off-kilter sets, the animatronic mask worn by the grotesque chief of police, Static Boy—and so much of it would have been impossible for any filmmaker lacking an effects or production design background. Given the current marketplace, so hostile towards independent filmmakers, it's a miracle that *Saint Bernard* received any distribution at all, let alone a wide release from the respected Severin Films label.

"I'm very conscious of what kind of films I'm making," Bartalos says. "It's true, the industry is changing radically, and the title 'independent film' has been hijacked by the majors. It's really rare to see a true independent film, and if it is being made, it's really hard for the filmmaker—the *auteur*—to really have a signature on it. I think, if nothing else, that's something I can offer to the projects I've been involved in, whether the music videos or short films I directed. And especially with my two feature films, *Skinned Deep* and *Saint Bernard*, I want it to have a flavor that is recognizable. That's probably the best aspect of doing a film independently. It's my ideas, my script. I'm literally hand-building and gleefully assembling everything. And, as much time as that takes up, the thing that's great is that doing all of that is a pleasure for me.

"There's nothing more fun for me than building a set for months to make it as deep and intricate as possible, as with the Uncle Eddie set at the end. That was done on my backyard porch, which allowed me every night, even when I'm exhausted from work, to spend a few hours screwing wood together. Every drive home, if I saw lumber being thrown out, I grabbed it—it was the ultimate recycling Greenpeace film. The entire process is something I really enjoy.

"And just like when you're sculpting a creature, your brain is analyzing it, cross-checking and spinning considerations like a Rubik's Cube and trying to find what's appropriate. When you're set-building, you're really taking a deep dive when you're hands-on. For me it's completely wonderful. It's a pure extension and almost the same as the makeup effects, visual pieces that the camera is going to point at. When I'm doing it myself, it's awesome, because I can literally set up the camera, put the lens on what I want to see, and see how that shot's gonna look."

Even the format was chosen deliberately. "The decision I made to shoot on film—there's a purity in the emulsion, so to speak," he says. "I felt that there was more of a message in the medium. If I'd shot this subject matter digitally, even with the careful transitions, there is a sort of cheapness to it, even when it's handled well. But, with film, people know, subconsciously, 'Shit, man, there are six or eight people standing around and there's a lot of money going through that thing!' I felt that legitimized it. When you point a motion picture camera at it, you'd be wise to do your homework and make sure everything you're shooting is exactly what you want it to be, which was the case with *Saint Bernard*.

"I actually think, since film is a tactile thing, and it's loaded on set, in an environment where people are there—happy, sad, pissed off, whatever—that energy somehow gets in there. That film is physically handled, it goes through a chemical bath, it goes through color grading, where it's loaded—I think that karmically, physically, the particles get in there. A high-end chef says that he won't cook for someone after he's had an argument with them because [the negativity] gets into the food. When you walk into a room after a couple's fucked or had a fight, you *feel*—you didn't see anything, you didn't hear anything—but you know 'Something just happened in here.' You pick up on that. I actually think film captures those microscopic, organic shed cells, and it gets in its DNA and helps form that. At its infancy, it captured something that it's able to radiate hopefully to the end."

The magic prevails because film, as a process—photo-chemical, art combined with science—is alchemy. *Saint Bernard* is a spell, one that took a long time to plan, shoot, and coordinate. "Once I had the film planned out," Bartalos says, "I wrote the script pretty quickly (in) about three to four months. I prepped for about eight months in building. I chose places where I could take the deep dive for the sets, like the police station was done at my studio, Atlantic West Effects. My backyard was used for the set for Uncle Ed. We shot on and off for about two-and-a-half years. We really wrapped all the shooting and the inserts and visual effects in 2015, then moved into the post-production audio elements—the complex sound design and beautiful music [by composer Dave Klotz]. Literally, right when I was done, I accepted the invitation for the Boston Underground Film Festival. So, that was its North American premiere in 2017. Then, things went really quickly to David Gregory at Severin Films, which I thought was a really good fit."

The modern-day indie filmmaker needs one thing—other than money, of course—and that's guts. All of *Saint Bernard* was planned out ahead of time, not unlike a heist, but luck had to be on their side as well.

In one sequence, shot in Paris without permits, Bernard lumbers around in a wooden suit. Bartalos explains: "When we went to Paris, I knew I needed Jay fully entombed in the wooden suit at that point. The setup was a sculptural gag. With the 5.7mm lens, as I pan up, the wood encrustation blends into the Eiffel Tower. What we did was we literally walked around the perimeter of the Eiffel Tower and timed the two guards with machine guns and the third guy that followed 10 feet behind them. We figured out that we had about four minutes and eight seconds after they turned the corner.

"So I'd prebuilt as much as I could of the wooden sculptural part, and then, when one guard's back was to us as he turned the corner, we could see down by the hedges and we quickly drywall-screwed Jay into this ornate wooden outfit. I had the camera all set up on the high-hat, and we shot it a few times before they came back around the corner. We had a limited time in France, and, if we didn't get that, they would have had their eyes out for us. Any problem would have sabotaged the shot."

For the critical sequence atop the overpass, another heist was planned. "Huge orchestration on our part," he says, "stopping traffic in Los Angeles, on the on-ramp where Jay discovers [the dog's] severed head. I wanted it to look epic, so that every other filmmaker goes, 'What the fuck?

That's *real*! That's not digital. They're really stopped!' So, I picked the busiest day of the year for traffic in L.A., the Monday after Easter. There's a notorious freeway exchange between the 118 and the 5 where you have this beautiful view of this nightmare traffic when you commute on rough days. So, we had four vehicles behind our car that gradually slowed traffic down.

"We'd rehearsed at five in the morning at my house, using little toy cars so everyone was clear what they were doing. No one else [in traffic] knew that our car was being followed by four production cars, which all began to slow down gradually so no one would get hurt. We slowly bought everyone around us to a dead stop and then the shooting sequence went into high gear. I followed Jay out of the vehicle with my camera on my shoulder with a fixed 9.2 lens. I positioned the bag, dressed it with blood, Jay went and picked it up. And the [picture car] just sat there idle while he walked down the ramp while I filmed him and did some reverse shots. And what's funny is most people were hoping to just get by this traffic jam, they weren't even paying attention to us. Obviously, when he walked by with the thing's spinal cord hanging out, they did a double-take.

"While my eye was on the lens, I'm telling you, I was thinking, 'This…is…*awesome*!' The expanse of seeing all those cars, it suggests that we had created this *other* jam! There's a wonderful back and forth about what you see, what you feel, what you internalize—it's really effective. If we didn't get that, or if a cop was close by or some commuter had decided to take a swing at me because they knew we were fucking around, that would have collapsed the day. It would have been annoying to try and figure out how to do it again. It would have been disheartening to think that I'd written something that really was out of reach. By the time I'd penned the sequence with plucked chickens parachuting out of airplanes, it was like, 'All right, now we're really pushing the limits of what we can get here.'"

Still, luck. "Luck was with us the whole time," he agrees. "*Skinned Deep* was trickier. I remember when we did the truck battle, where the crazy family battles the guys in the pickup. Initially, we just couldn't get a break. We went out there with all these people, including Warwick Davis from England, to barren roads we'd scouted out in Palmdale, no one around, perfect to go fast and shoot

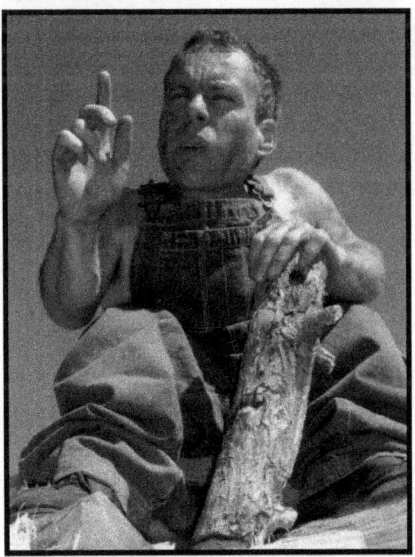

Legendary Warwick Davis as Othello, Bernard's Virgil. (Think about that one for a minute.)

33

some ambitious footage of vehicles battling on the open road. But we ran into some jackoff piece of shit city/county worker sitting there, probably masturbating and avoiding his real work, who had nothing better to do, once he realized we wanted to film, than to follow us around and make life Hell. Any side road we went down and hopped to get lost, an hour later this idiot would find us and try to execute some form of petty assigned authority."

Catastrophe looms on any set. When you shoot guerrilla-style, you further buck the odds and Film Gods. For one sequence in *Skinned Deep*, Dugre, as Brain, fantasizes about being free, and, in his mind, "freedom" means a naked jog down a busy city street.

"That was a tough thing to get," says Bartalos, "and, unfortunately, Jay wound up doing some jail time for that [overnight]. We had a wonderful vantage point from various places on a building top and on the street, we had a van waiting, and we'd rehearsed it. We'd done some walkthroughs. You know, God bless Jay Dugre, he was willing to go full nude with the brain, to really just radiate the ultimate in freedom.

"He did it once and it was fine. Then, we put on a different lens and what we found out later was that two lady undercover cops had seen a blur of flesh. They waited and sure enough, when we did it again, they tackled Jay. And, when I went running over, I didn't know they were cops. So, when I went to pull them off of him, they looked at me like I was insane! I'm pulling their arms—and then the badges came out! "Whoa, sorry!" We had a robe, and Jay was in the robe with nothing else—butt-ass naked in the van—down to the police station. And they kept him overnight.

"It was funny—he said the most compromising moment of his entire life was that he couldn't fit in the van with the brain on, so he had to shimmy down in his seat. So, he says the robe opens up, his nuts are hanging out, he's got the brain on. At this point, the cops are laughing at him. He's handcuffed! Down at the station, the vibe changed. He said everyone was laughing and taking pictures, but then they told him to take the brain off. And he said, 'Well, I kind of can't.' It's glued on; there's what's called the core, and he was blended in. Then, he said, for some reason, they got spooked—like maybe there was a bomb in it and he was a kind of Trojan horse!

"And then the vibe got completely dark. They pulled and peeled it off and saw the headpiece was hollow. Then, they took his shoelaces so he wouldn't hang himself. He unfortunately had to stay overnight until we could bail him out the next morning. The thing is, I don't even think they realized it was for a film! He said they kind of just thought he was a crazy nudist that liked to make himself up or something, which is even funnier! Why else would this knucklehead be doing this?

"I think I saw more dimensions to Jay's acting then, and he was excited to come back [for *Saint Bernard*]. He's a true actor; he loves to explore boundaries and limitations and how to get past them. I give him a lot of credit because he's stone-faced and, in a sense, being the public.

Playing the blank slate is harder than one imagines. He needed very little guidance as we went along. He's a very good actor, and we had a good time all through it. I was glad he had so much fun with it, because it was a demanding role. He was in every element—water, wind, sun, a lot of difficult stuff—all the way through and he never flinched. He's excellent."

Acting, in a film that is so disjointed, is crucial to keeping up the façade. Any missteps would eject the viewer clear out of the rabbit hole. While Bernard is our Virgil through this madness, Dugre encounters some horrible people played by wonderful performers.

Take, for example, Bob Zmuda, the notorious companion of Andy Kaufman who shared Kaufman's lounge-singer character, the unctuous Tony Clifton, and assumed the role after the comedian's death. Playing Clifton required extensive makeup for both men, and both disappeared into the role upon donning the costume. "When I see Bob [Zmuda] becoming the Tony Clifton character," says Bartalos, "I'm kind of stunned, because he shape-shifts. He literally goes from this one guy to this other person who happens to know how to shuffle and dance. And I'm like, 'What the fuck? That's so weird!' The masquerade of the prosthetics allows for another person.

"And this goes back to what we were talking about. Is this something that was dormant in Bob as an entertainer and he found his place with Andy, a way for him to keep exercising that, because it's pleasurable through this masquerade? Because you don't just go, 'Oh, this is my gig; I gotta carry the torch and learn that stuff.' It's too advanced, having that sense of theater where he can turn on a dime. He knows cinematic beats and timing. So, when I asked him to be the priest in *Saint Bernard*, who's kind of sleazy and money-grubbing, he laughed and got it and was happy to join in. I think he really nails it, especially when he gets frustrated with Bernard and turns into the monster priest."

Bartalos has had a healthy working relationship with Warwick Davis, famed star of *Willow* and the *Leprechaun* series. Davis appears in *Saint Bernard* as one of the very few benevolent visions. "Working with Warwick on *Leprechaun*, he totally brought that character to life and he was great," he says. "When you're on set, watching an actor get ready, you see what is written in the script and what the scenario asks. And then I'd watch Warwick turn his acting talents on—he totally owns it and gives it the flare. He completely understood its place and how to play it.

"That's what a studio looks for in a franchise character, an entity, its own thing. That's what makes a really fulfilled thespian actor. Plates is the perfect starting point—I wrote all these really absurd lines and whacked-out scenarios, and he completely legitimized it. We had discussions about it, he internalized it, and when the cameras rolled, he exploded as Plates and it was great!

"So, Othello in *Saint Bernard* is more reserved character; it's more nuanced but no less odd. He wanted to know the baseline, 'What does he mean to you? Give me a hint.' I said, 'Really, Warwick, you represent a guardian angel to him. You pop up in the film—Bernard is going through a rough time, you appear, you're a good guy, and you grant him some time. That's what he is; he's a positive force.' I said, 'If there was any place for mysticism in this film, like 0.01 [percent], it would be here.' It's really cool how he can internalize those lines and get it right to the perfect level. I can't say enough good things about Warwick."

The most surprising thing about *Saint Bernard*, given its story, structure, and presentation, is how well it's been received by the film-watching community. Horror buffs, surrealism fans, cult fanatics have all embraced this marvelously wacky, inventive, scatological, disturbing work of art.

Says Bartalos: "I'm really pleased about the response. The divisive nature of the film is not lost on me; I probably wear it on my sleeve. I would rather make a film that a smaller population really likes than make something that compromises the uniqueness I could bring to a film for a mass audience. That being said, as more and more people like it, I'm not pretending that I don't like it. I really

Another great shot of The Chief.

find that encouraging. When it is such a singular vision, there's that danger of it being too homegrown and too personal, and it doesn't connect.

"At the same time, from my years in the industry, I think I have a good sense that, even when I'm introducing outrageous and graphic elements, I'd rather have people look at the screen than cover their eyes and look away. I've always wondered about that. You chop off a head and someone turns away—you just missed the effect I spent months on! I'd rather find a way to make it palatable, especially if I can challenge their sensibilities. That seems to be exactly what's happening. When some people don't connect with it, that's fine. I've actually gone out of my way to make it nonlinear and at times fragmented, but it is a narrative that unfolds through an emotional level, communicated primarily through a mosaic of abstract scenarios.

"I firmly believe that, as strong as our literary skills are, there is still no match to the power of creative imagery. It's very, very flattering and exciting that people are responding positively to *Saint Bernard*. That's important to me—it's not meant to exist in a vacuum. It may be that for people who don't know why they're connecting with it. It could be because its fragmented narrative style isn't that alien. It's actually very close to the way their subconscious works, but people haven't put a spotlight on it or portrayed storytelling that way before or had it explained to them— the way you are connected is actually the way you're thinking right now. You're thinking about three things while you're doing this and that— that's how your brain works; it's a wonderful thing!"

Pick up *Saint Bernard* on Blu-ray from Severin Films.

Director and madman, Gabe Bartalos.

THE WISDOM AND SYNCHRONICITY OF
CARMINE CAPOBIANCO
by Dr. Rhonda Baughman

I took Capobianco at his word when, after our first interview, he whispered: *Call me again if you need another interview. I got stories for days.*

All right, so that's not *exactly* verbatim and he didn't *really* whisper but he *did* say he'd had a lovely time during out interview and wouldn't mind me reaching out again when I asked if I could pester him in the future for a part two. Additionally, I liked that he always has something prolific on his mind; the man might pretend he's thinking about waffles on a cute Tuesday Facebook pic, but chat with him for five minutes and you'll know better. In addition to the waffles, the star of *Psychos in Love* and *Galactic Gigolo*, whose acting career found resurgence in recent years, probably thinking about world peace, cinema, family, and friends. The man has stamina. The man has energy.

Carmine's not at 100% and feels the need to apologize. I follow him on social media (as a fan and devoted acolyte, not a stalker) and I can see there are a few serious health issues dogging him. Unfairly, I might add—it's time for the universe to cut him some slack. I tell him there's no need to even consider apologizing and if there's anything at all any of us can do to help him on his way to a speedy recovery, just say the word and we shall do it. He has numerous loved ones—family and friends and fans—who keep him front and center in their good thoughts for the day ritual, myself among them.

"When I got a nurse with a great sense of humor, one who really understood my own humor, I really felt a lot better. It was a turning point for the day. She was able to understand my need to joke about strange and uncomfortable things," he says. [RB note: think stool and lycanthropes, or don't, or just visit Carmine's FB page—he tells it way better than I ever could.] "But really, the day I was in a room full of people, taking in some serious drugs, and the doctor comes in and jokingly, affectionately and says to everyone around me while waggling a finger: *be careful of this guy.* There was laughter and a genuine sense or respect and good reputations all around. It was another positive turning point," Carmine says.

I'll be brutally honest here: for a man who has just finished another round of chemo, he's in amazingly good spirits, sounds positive and upbeat, and if he hadn't been so forthright about his condition to

Carmine Capobianco as Eoj Oilgamert (that's Joe Tremaglio backwards. Yes, it's funny.) Courtesy Carmine Capobianco.

those of us who follow him online, we may have never known. I'm glad he told us, however, I want him to know he's not alone—and there's no need to be silent. Because there is more than just hope—there's meds and procedures and statistics and remission. I believe all of this strongly, firmly, one hundred percently.

It should be noted, too, that Carmine handles health difficulties the same as he handles hecklers in post-screening chats and in convention panels: in stride, with grace and his usual good humor. He notes after one showing of *Psychos in Love:* "It was a great copy the theater had gotten a hold of and it looked good on the big screen. There's always going to be that one guy in the audience trying to ruin everyone's good time," Carmine says.

I get it. Any boring hater taking the time to heckle is probably a pretty miserable person in real life. But to interrupt MY good time with boorish behavior? Ah, hell no. I'd have fought him.

"There were a lot of pictures taken that night and I have a lot of great memories. That heckler was going to ruin absolutely nothing," Carmine says.

"I don't even have to ask if you still get recognized before a show or even while out and about," I say. "What I want to know is: do you still get excited when fans approach?"

"Oh, absolutely. I get an emotional chubby when recognized. Recently, when I was recognized, the fan told me that he has a new girlfriend and it might last. See, after a couple of dates, he shows his potential lifemate *Psychos in Love* and if she doesn't get it, he says goodbye. I thought for sure he was joking, but after studying the look on his face? Nope. I would have to say he was 100% serious. I sure hope it works out for those crazy kids. Another fan, this one was from Australia, created a drinking game from *Galactic Gigolo*. I will always love to hear from fans," he says. "You know, I also hear from people who say they saw *Psychos* long after it came out and that it was simply because Blockbuster couldn't carry it," Carmine says. "Blockbuster could carry *Gigolo*, though, and it's all simply due to ratings. *Psychos* was Unrated and *Gigolo* had the R."

"Maybe that's why they went under?" I suggest. "But they so still have someone running the so-sad-it's-funny Twitter account called The Last Blockbuster."

Carmine is probably more familiar with those bizarre intricacies of the ratings system than I am; he was the proprietor of FunStuff, his own video store chain[1], for many years. His youngest daughter is carrying on the family tradition. "She currently works at a non-profit in Hamden at Best Video[2] which also has coffee

---

1   *https://archives.rep-am.com/2012/09/11/somehow-they-survive/*
2   *https://www.bestvideo.com*

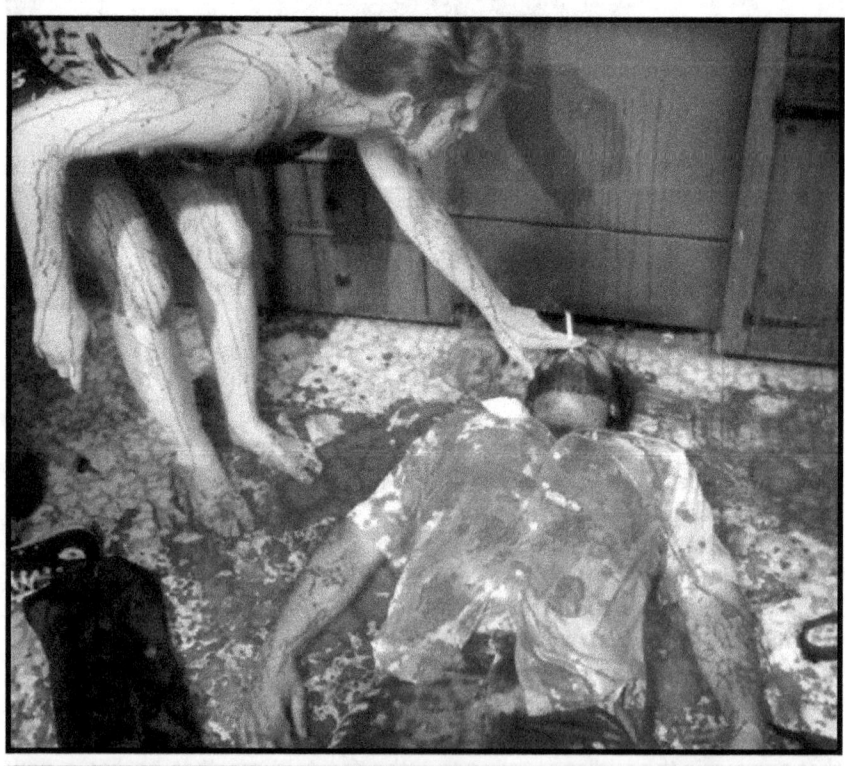

Debi Thibault wore many hats on the set of Psychos in Love.
Photo Courtesy Gorman Bechard.

and shows and all kinds of other live events," he says.

Once over squealing that there are others on the planet that understand that the video store goes much further than simple nostalgia (community, for example), our conversation turns to his viewing habits. Carmine is not one to sit still, but I thought perhaps while he was healing, he may fallen down one of those streaming service rabbit holes that occasionally even tangle the best of us, because like me, he's also given up on regular TV since the commercials are beyond mind-numbing in the 21st century.

"I hated losing the flow in a show when the commercials came. Interruptive and repetitive. I got hooked on *The Exorcist, Elementary, Brooklyn 99, Goldbergs*, and *Family Matters*. The time was right for me to find that last one. The comedic presence and timing of [Jaleel White as] Steve Urkel is phenomenal. I watched the cast reunion and the '90s was a long time ago for me to recall such details, but apparently, you couldn't go anywhere without seeing *Family Matters* merchandise and advertising. And while Urkel may have gotten annoying to a lot of people, his part originally began as just a walk-on but the response to him was so great, they brought him back and the rest is now history to stream. I'm going on record to say how amazing I think that show is," Carmine says. If there's anyone who would know about comedic timing, it's Capobianco. "And I've also been doing a lot of reading. I have a decent number of doctor appointments, too, so I've developed a new taste for audio books," he says. "There are a few, too, from Stephen King, for example, that made it to I couldn't wait to get in the car. That's talent."

Carmine latest project is the written word, a soon-to-be-released book, illustrated by friends and fans. "It's really more like a page a year I've written and saved over the last thirty years, so don't get too excited until you read it," he laughs. "I've recently taken a break from horror, too—I decided to so with a new author to me, so I chose Nicholas Sparks, and wound up loving it."

"Tell me more about this thirty pages. Is it poetry?" I ask.

"I definitely don't do poetry," he says. "Unless, well, maybe a few here and there, for girlfriends over the years. I'd make sure they'd know it was all *just* for them, like, of course, 'baby, I wrote this *just for you*'," he says. I have to laugh because what girl hasn't fallen for that bit? Myself included. Ugh.

"For real, it started with my editor from my local newspaper. He let me have the freedom to write what I wanted.[3] So, whenever I had a little bit of free time, I'd scribble here and there, send a few things his way over the years. He appreciated the things I wrote, articles, shorts, I guess. But this thing I'll send to you—I'm not sure what it is," he says. "If anything, it reminds me of a joke someone once told me that wasn't funny, not exactly—and it was long but not tedious, and I'm just almost choking with laughter, almost crying, kind of a choke-cry thing and it feels good. Really good. So, yeah I want people

3   *I have one of those, too! Thanks, MW!*

to react to any book I'd write that way. And when it's done, I imagine it will need an illustrator," Carmine says. So, he *has* thought of what a finished product might look like—and I tell him that's how writers think, so he's well on his way whatever the words may be and whatever form they may take.

Our conversation swings back to movies, sequels in particular. I mention the film that double-billed with his *Galactic Gigolo*, one *Sorority Babes in the Slimeball Bowl-O-Rama* (and one of my favorite films of all time for many reasons), has a sequel in the works—teaming Brinke Stevens and David DeCoteau once more. And I ask Carmine if anyone has ever approached him about a remake or a sequel to *Psychos*.

"There's been several sequel discussions and even a few things written in the past, but none that has come to fruition," Carmine says. [*Hey, we gave it a shot!—Ed.*] "We didn't want to re-hash the same thing. The things we had been given to review didn't feel original enough, so we just didn't move forward with it. It was like trying to add to *Casablanca* or *Star Wars* or *Rocky Horror*—and I'm not comparing my movie to those, believe me, but thy worked in such a way that there was nothing to add. Folks did in two of those cases, but there was no need. People are still watching all of those aforementioned movies, they're still watching *Psychos in Love*, and more importantly, they're enjoying it. I'm with John Huston on this one—why don't we remake some of our bad movies—remake the ones that *need* another shot, you know? Remake them and make them better;

try it again, and if it still sucks, well then, go on to something else," he says.

I know Carmine is a busy, busy man, so I thank him for his time and I think he hears my genuine appreciation for this afternoon's vox (insert more Latin here if needed), as well as for his wisdom and synchronicity—and while he doesn't scream in ecstasy about that idea of a third interview with the foundation hovering near his time with Funstuff Video—he doesn't veto it either! Excellent! I'll let him chill and recover a bit before I start firing those questions at him, however. I'll need him well-rested, at peak CC form for that vision quest. In the mean-time, this gives readers time to catch up on/review all movies Capobianco: I recommend starting with *Galactic Gigolo* before *Psychos in Love* and then hitting *Model Hunger* after those two *and then* going hard at all the remaining films on his IMDB[4] profile. I'm willing to bet there is a goldmine of synchronicity among the films between *Gigolo* and *Hunger* and Capobianco's time at his Funstuff Video Store location. I've got images and questions swirling in my head about those halcyon days and you can feel free to email me them if you'd like me to ask for you—OR you can follow this rabbit hole footnote[5] and see where it leads for you: I'll see you down there.

---

4   https://www.imdb.com/name/nm0135292/?ref_=nv_sr_1?ref_=nv_sr_1

5   http://www.carminecapobianco.com/

PSYCHOS IN LOVE (1987)

Joe owns a bar; Kate is a lonely manicurist. Both long for love, for understanding, but find both difficult to achieve. It makes them angry, frustrated, forlorn. Eventually, their paths cross and it's love at first sight, particularly because they share one crucial personality trait: they're both psychopathic murderers. Love, happiness, hilarity and gore ensues.

Over the last twenty-some years, Gorman Bechard's *Psychos in Love* has developed a devoted and deserved cult following. It's a movie that's incredibly easy to like, despite the outwardly-lurid subject matter. It's a black comedy that owes more than a little debt to Paul Bartel's 1982 *Eating Raoul*. But hands-down the reason it works is due to the natural chemistry of stars Carmine Capobianco and Debi Thibeault. It's easy to believe that these two star-crossed crazies would fall for each other because, first and foremost, they like each other. Homicidal tendencies aside, they enjoy just hanging out and being silly together, and the non-cynical viewer will enjoy hanging out with them as well. The pair reteamed with Bechard for the additional outings *Galactic Gigolo* and *Cemetery High* as part of a multi-picture deal with Charles Band's now-defunct Empire Pictures, but neither of those work quite as well or possess the goofy charm of *Psychos in Love*.

Shot on 16mm for just $75,000, the finished film has a strange documentary quality to it, *Man Bites Dog* if the central characters were jovial. Make no mistake, the low budget makes itself known: the camerawork is rough as is the sound, Capobianco performs the score on a Casio keyboard (the "*Psychos* Love Theme" performed by Carmine and Debi is as funny and earnest as the rest of the film), and most of the other performers are, well, less than stellar. The gore is fun and the story never gets boring, but if you grew up raised on the flawless offerings of Hollywood, the inner joy of *Psychos in Love* may leave you behind. Many of the humorless slugs that slime the Internet message boards have of course branded this as "worst movie ever" just moments before declaring something else to be "worst movie ever." Yes, the slimmest of dimes spent is visible on the screen, but so is every bit of love put in.

But Joe, Kate, and the rest of the characters exist in *Psychos in Love* world, of course, and *Psychos in*

Love is fully aware that it is a movie. The fourth wall is gleefully broken as often as possible—Capobianco, a die-hard Groucho fan, delivers a "strange interlude" midway through the film while the rest of the cast waits patiently. This "movie reality" gives the filmmakers a lot of leeway, which is good news for its limited budget. If an effect doesn't land—or worse, if a joke doesn't land—the *unreality* has already said, "this isn't real, this is a movie, we're doing this for you." There's nothing dishonest about *Psychos in Love*. It wants to be irreverent, funny, gory, and do so with a touch of heart. To those ends, the movie exceeds its goal. Why else would we even be talking about it?

The couple's shared rant—"*I hate grapes! I hate green grapes. I hate purple grapes. I hate grapes with seeds. I hate grapes without seeds. I hate them separately, in bunches and in little groups of twos and threes. I fucking hate grapes!*"—is occasionally heard chanted at horror conventions by "those in the know," much like a verbal secret handshake. Though the rant itself—one of the pair's given reasons for their murderous impulses—was a throwaway gag Capobianco and Bechard came up with during the first draft of the script. It's a meaningless MacGuffin, but it's still very funny.

Even better, Joe and Kate's relationship evolves as well. At one point, the pair grow bored with murder and decide to just settle down. Of course, living in a movie world, comfortable complacency is never rewarded and soon too-deserving victims pop up again. And this is just as important as the gags and laughs. We grow to really *like* Kate and Joe. Horror fans, having grown up with movies exploiting the worst-case cinematic scenario, have a tendency to fear for the worst, and I've talked to a number of people who discovered *Psychos* for the first time and felt a sense of dread throughout, fearing that Joe and Kate would be gunned down in the final frames ala the Firefly clan in *The Devil's Rejects* or "name a character" in '70s crime films. But—*spoiler alert*—this is one story about unrepentant murderers that has a happy ending.

HER NAME WAS CHRISTA, HIS NAME IS LONNIE: THE RETURN OF JAMES L. EDWARDS

While his friends call him "Lonnie," most fans of '90s indie horror know him as James L. Edwards. A staple personality from filmmaker J.R. Bookwalter's considerable oeuvre, Lonnie appeared or starred in more than a dozen of Bookwalter's productions, including *Ozone*, *Polymorph* (which he wrote), *Robot Ninja*, and *The Sandman*. He's even a cruel running gag in Bookwalter's *Bad Movie Police* series, in which he's listed among the films' "crimes."

But he gave an oddly touching portrayal of serial killer Butch Harlow, who finds his soulmate, in Matt Walsh's *Bloodletting*, costarring Ariauna Albright. The 1997 shot-on-video black comedy has been favorably compared to Oliver Stone's *Natural Born Killers* in its portrayal of the unhinged as budding celebrities, with Lonnie and Ariauna's chemistry at the forefront. While *Bloodletting* turned out to be the swan song for the friendship of many of those involved—for a variety of reasons, both big and petty—the film resonated with audiences and fans.

"The idea [for *Her Name Was Christa*] came about out of my desire to do bigger projects," says Edwards. "I had semi-retired at that point. I was married and had kids. One of the reasons someone falls in love with you is because you're an actor, and then you get married and they don't want you to act because it takes time away from the family. Cut to me getting a divorce, me deciding to get back into this. But the problem was, while I'm always grateful for the roles I get, I wasn't getting the kinds of roles I wanted to play. I finally said, 'Fuck it, let's go ahead and plan my comeback movie.'"

Edwards sat down and worked on a script about Stephen, who is desperately lonely, and all he wants is companionship. A work colleague suggests he hire a prostitute and pay her for 'the girlfriend experience.' Anyone familiar with horror knows this relationship isn't going to end with a dance number and a wedding.

After wrapping the script in late 2016, Edwards turned towards financing. "I had a little bit of money set aside," he says, "but we still didn't have enough money in my opinion to do the script I'd written. So, we ran an Indiegogo and it was a historic failure. We wanted to raise 10 grand and I think we raised just over a grand. But I was determined. We basically had to streamline the script. Every favor I could think of I pulled for this movie. The upshot is we got the thing finished, we got it in under budget, and I'm extremely happy with the film."

When it came time to shoot, an actress that Lonnie had worked with back in the Tempe days—name withheld to avoid embarrassment or hurt feelings (shit happens!)—was set to play Christa, but creative differences arose. Not wanting to delay, Edwards made the decision to start shooting. He explains: "The only person who shares screen time with Christa is Stephen. I was able to go in and shoot everyone else's scenes. We'd shot six days, nearly everything in the script that didn't involve Christa." The bulk of the film, sans the character of Christa, wound up "in the can" before it became clear that the intended would be unable to participate. Lonnie was faced with the uncomfortable conclusion that they'd have to recast.

Returning to the audition process was a hardship for the production and not a small pain to deal with. Before the "Christa" search, filming had been humming along smoothly, with the bulk of the cast coming from unusual sources.

Says Lonnie, "Drew Fortier, who played Stephen's only sympathetic co-worker, Nick, was just a fan who had contacted me on Facebook and had said he wanted to work with me. He asked if he could audition for me, I said great. I sent him the sides, and he literally sent in his audition eight minutes later. He'd obviously never acted before, but he's a musician; he played with Chuck Mosley from Faith No More. I told him, 'I have to be honest with you, your read was terrible. But I like your look and I think you can do this. I think the problem is you rushed yourself. Take a week, think about the sides, and send me another audition.' And, a week later, I got the audition and he was phenomenal. I asked him

Lonnie as Stephen.

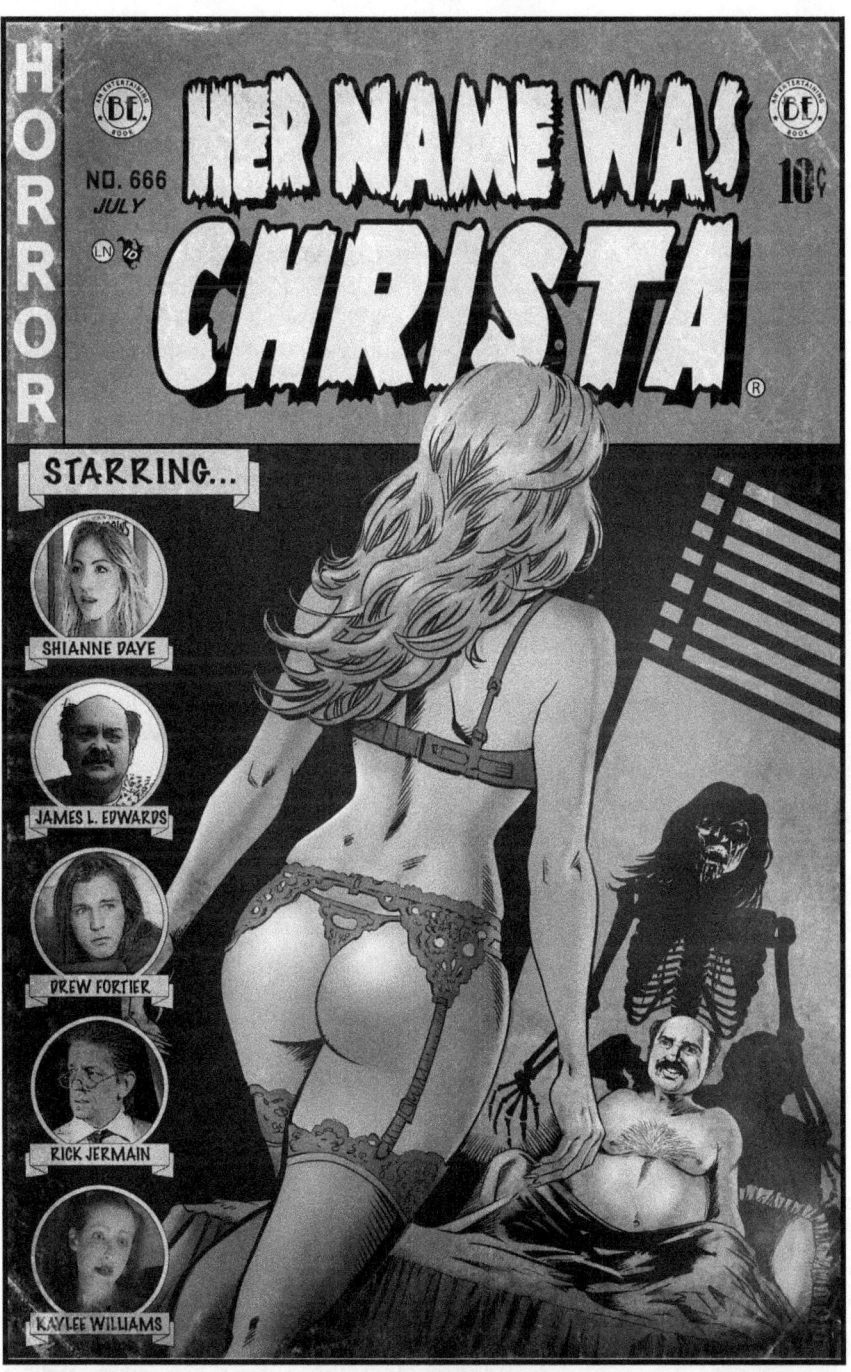

"CHRISTA" teaser art - all photos copyright and courtesy James L. Edwards.

The Marvelous Scooter McCrae and the Transcendent Sasha Graham in CHRISTA.

to come in and meet me. So, I met him at Chuck Mosley's house!

"I'd met Rick Jermain, who plays Stephen's boss, Blaze, on the set of Brad Twigg's *Killer Campout*. We were rivals in that film—he was a sheriff and I was a bounty hunter. I liked working with him. When we thought we had a budget, we were talking to a couple of people who represented John Waters to play the role of Blaze. It never got any farther than conversation—I don't think Waters was even made aware of it.

"Another name this representative floated by us, for Nick, was Corey Feldman, who was at the time within what we thought our budget was going to be. I'd heard all the nightmare stories about working with him, but I was like, 'Fuck, it's Corey Feldman! I have to do this!' But the week before we were going to try and make this happen, he had his *Today Show* appearance, and the next time I talked to his rep, his asking price had multiplied by 10. So, we stopped all negotiations. Drew and Rick were the better choices and they worked out great."

But the key and title role was still unfound. According to Edwards, "We took six months off—three months of recasting, then another two months set aside for [the new Christa] and me to basically break down the script, and we went over it and over it. When we were looking for a new Christa, we completely saturated the area. We'd auditioned 73 actresses from all over the United States, a couple from Canada and one from Germany, only to find Shianne Daye just 10 minutes down the road from my house! That was just phenomenal. Shianne Daye showed up, I realized, 'This is Christa. This is who I'd been looking for.' I definitely count luck among the elements that allowed us to cast Christa.

"I'd purposely cast people I'd either worked with in the past or who I was familiar with, with the exception of Shianne. Shianne was fresh out of the box, had done some print work and modeling, but she told me ahead of time, 'I'm probably not going to get this role because usually directors don't like my voice.' [Daye's voice is indeed unique, both high and breathy at the same time.] But that was a selling point for me. I have a unique voice, and she has a unique voice. I think that our chemistry together improves because of them. Shianne was the very last person I'd auditioned.

"What I learned from that was that this actress had an incredible ability to absorb dialogue, she was really good—anybody can memorize

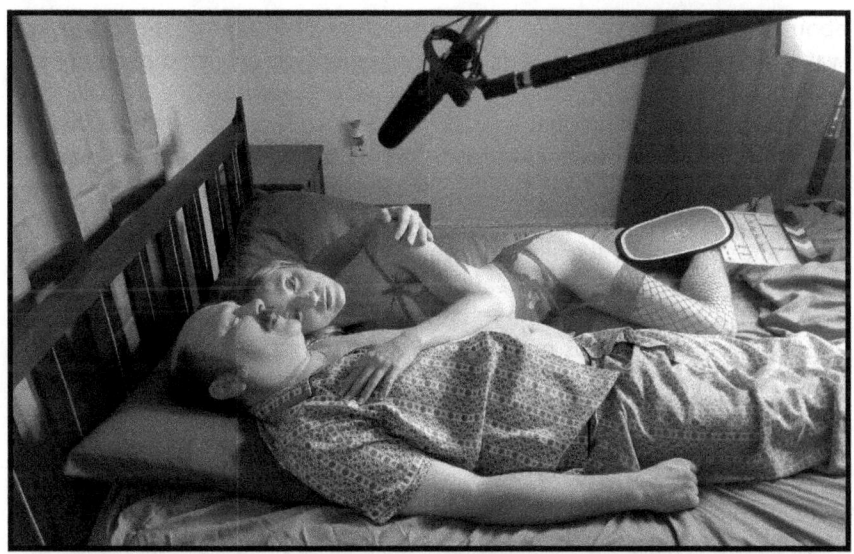

Stephen and Christa (Shianne Daye) share a quiet moment with a boom mike and the slate. (Don't be silly, it's a behind-the-scenes of CHRISTA.)

dialogue, but to capture the emotion of that dialogue takes a lot of work. I will say, right off the bat, my main concern was if there was going to be chemistry. You can have two very accomplished actors, but if there's no chemistry between them, that can ruin a film. I was fortunate enough to take those two months of rehearsal. We were able to get to know each other's strengths and weaknesses and go from there.

"Obviously, I had to rewrite parts of the script once we cast Shianne Daye. I only had to tweak it slightly, actually. The script went from Christa being an older—I don't want to say 'over the hill,' but an older prostitute. Shianne is quite a bit younger. There were some subplot elements we had to get rid of with Shianne being younger, things like Christa getting into hooking after she got too old to strip."

Her Name Was Christa doesn't glamorize anything—not the prostitution, not the dead-end life Stephen leads. In fact, Edwards' character is as far removed from a "typical" leading man as you can get. When you get down to it, *Christa* is an actor's movie. For the audience to buy into the situation, it's imperative that they connect with the characters and even fall in love with them. It's crucial that you sympathize with Stephen and Christa, given where their relationship winds up. The tragedy comes before the horror.

Says Edwards, "Again, while I'm always grateful for the work I get, it's been a long time since I played a role I was really passionate about. One of the exceptions was Butch Harlow. But, let's be honest, Butch Harlow is 'What if Lonnie became a serial killer?'— Matt [Walsh] said as much when he wrote it—whereas this gave me the opportunity to create a character and show emotion. You can say a lot about me, but you can't say *Christa* was a vanity piece. I purposely gained weight for the role, I'm bald in the role, it's not a flattering character at all. I want this to be very human and real.

"Even in the casting of Shianne, while she's beautiful, it's almost like a girl-next-door obtainable beauty. I was so tired of seeing movies that are casting these obvious models as prostitutes—that's not how real life works. I wanted Christa to be beaten down by life and confront the foreign concept of someone actually wanting to love and care for her. One of the problems I've always had with indie films, and with horror in general, is they're never interested in exploring characters to any great degree, and they end up being meat props. If I see a woman stabbed to death in a movie, that's horrific. But if I see a woman whose backstory I know, who I've invested emotionally in as a character, and then she's stabbed, I feel a thousand times worse. That's just Filmmaking 101."

Lonnie continues, "I had a lot of things to prove with this project. One of the reasons I wanted desperately to play an incredibly humbled figure is because back in the time of, say, Alternative Cinema and *Bloodletting* and *Polymorph*, I was—and I completely admit this—an arrogant asshole, to be quite frank. I freely admit that. I was a pain in the ass to work with on set because I thought I was hot shit. At the end of the day, it's like, 'Dude, you're doing little shot-on-video movies. You're not Brad Pitt.' But, somehow, I'd acquired this incredible ego.

"And one of the things I wanted to show in this movie is that age and experience is an incredibly humbling fucking creature. One of the best reviews I ever got as an actor, *I thought* at the time—though looking back at it it's one of the most horrifying things I'd ever read—from my old Tempe days, someone had done a review of, I believe it was *Bloodletting*. They had said, 'James L. Edwards always plays the same character in every movie, but that's OK because James L. Edwards is an interesting guy to get to know.' And at the time I thought, 'Oh, that's cool,' but now realize no, that's a horrible fucking thing to say. It's basically saying that I'm not an actor, I'm a personality, and that's not what I ever intended to be.

"My directing this film was out of necessity only. I don't have any aspirations to be a director. This was just a project I was incredibly passionate about. I had intended to hire a director, but, unfortunately, I think what I'd wanted was to hire a 'yes man.' I wanted to hire someone

POLYMORPH's Lonnie and Sasha reunited.

who would put their name on the movie but direct it my way, which wasn't the right thing to do. I'd interviewed several directors for this, and, of course, all of them wanted to put their own personal stamp on the project—why wouldn't you want to do that? That didn't jive with what I wanted, and I had to be honest and say, 'Fuck it, I'll do it myself.' And, by finally accepting that I was going to direct, that became one more thing I had to prove."

So, for his first big project in a decade, Lonnie placed hurdles in his path, then set them on fire. Not only was he taking on a challenging and unglamorous role, he was assuming the mantle of director as well. Directing others is a headache; directing yourself can be a nightmare. "I'll be honest with you," he says. "I went into this with a very naïve standpoint. 'Well, shit, I've acted in plenty of things, I'll be fine.' But I was going into this in a role that I was very adamant to prove that I could sell. I'd gotten it into my head, because of that one review, 'You're not an actor, you're a personality.' I was very hungry to prove myself.

"But you have to be careful when you know you're going to direct yourself. You put yourself into the mindset of this humble, meek character, and then, when you call 'Cut,' you have to be in charge. That was tough, that was the bitch of the bunch. I had to put up a front at all times. The last thing you want to communicate to your crew is that you don't have any control. When I was an actor, the first time a director showed me he wasn't in complete control, I'd lose respect. Not to be a dick, but it happens. 'Yeah, you're playing this broken character, but guess what? Everything that happens on set is your responsibility. If this gets fucked up, you've got nobody to blame but yourself. So, good luck, kid.'"

The break in filming resulted in a rather schizophrenic production team, he recalls. "I ended up having two crews on this film. The first was during the initial six days of shooting, after which everyone except for my producer ended up disappearing. One of the worst things you can do on an indie film is have long periods of time between shooting, especially when people are volunteering their time. Everyone wants to work on a movie until it comes time to work on the movie, because it's a lot of *work*.

"The majority of the crew I had at the beginning, except for Keith Kline [first assistant camera and friend of *E.N.*], had no film experience whatsoever. While I was incredibly grateful for their time, there weren't too many—I didn't lose much more than bodies when it came time to go back. Keith was a different animal. It was just an unfortunate situation when he got sick. Keith was with me from the very early stages of Indiegogo; he came aboard as director of photography. I enjoyed working with him a lot. There were a series of unfortunate situations that arose when he had to depart the film."

If you've seen the poster—or grokked the title—you can guess the direction *Christa* travels. At some point, you're going to see Stephen in bed with a corpse. The film doesn't skimp on the gore in this regard, and the third act really requires the viewer to be on board with Stephen and

Christa's relationship. Essential to this was veteran effects artist Al Tuskes (*The Rage*, *Face Off*) and his movie magic.

"Al Tuskes was fantastic," says Lonnie. "He was a real joy to work with. Once he read the script, I said, 'I'm going to shoot the sex scenes as romantic, but as graphic as possible. I don't want it to jump the border between racy and pornographic, but I want it to come close.' As erotic and showy as those love scenes are, I want to do the exact same thing with the 'reality' ones, in a grotesque 'what-the-hell-is-happening' context.' I'm basically expecting the audience to care about this character so much that when it comes to those scenes, they say, 'This is really grotesque, but I get why he's doing it.' That's the hardest part of this film."

These scenes will certainly be challenging to the viewer. Neither Lonnie nor Tuskes pulls any punches when showing the degradation of a decomposing body. "I've had people react to the gruesomeness of the reality of the sex scenes, but as far as the actual portrayal, it's in no way gratuitous or pornographic. It's essential to the story," he says. Which is true. The story's natural progression and buildup make these final sequences important to Stephen's (and Christa's) evolution, and Edwards films these sequences in a remarkable way that will leave audiences both enthralled and repulsed.

Unfortunately, due to the nature of horror and the marketplace, distributors focus more on the climax than the lead-up, which is, in this instance, the wrong way around. Says Edwards: "What cracks me up is that a lot of people see this as I made a

FX maestro Al Tuskes doing...something.

Work, Work, Work.

'corpse-fucking movie.' No. If you think all this is just a 'corpse-fucking movie,' you've completely missed the point of it. The horror part of this movie is about getting older and becoming obsolete and dying alone. Just the idea of the extremes someone will go to ensure they're not alone is what this film is really about. Part of the thing I'm fighting with distributors right now is [that] they want to slap a *Nekromantik* image on the cover, and I'm like, 'You're totally missing the fucking point.'"

Which is sad, though understandable to an extent. It's easier to sell a "corpse-fucking film" than "aging schlub finds love in madness."

Lonnie adds, "I met with a foreign rep who said, 'We love the movie, but we want you to cut it by a minimum of 15 minutes, we can't tell you where to cut it, and we want to change the cover and change the name.' I'm like, 'Absolutely not. I'm not doing that.'

"'Well,' he said, 'it's the difference between 1,000 people seeing your movie and 100 people seeing it.'

"Having 1,000 people see my movie does me no good if 800 are angry and feeling duped. They don't care. They don't care about your second movie. They just want to make money off your first one."

The edict to cut is also an understandable reaction. Most indie horror runs a clean 80 minutes. *Christa* takes its time, building the drama before lurching into the horror. "I never intended to make a two-hour movie," Edwards claims. "For the most part, the script is intact. We cut one scene and it was one I fought really hard about. I'm of the opinion that you need an exploding head in your movie in the first 10 minutes. I really believe that. *Christa* doesn't have that.

"But it did initially. Right after the title sequence, there's a scene where Stephen wakes up screaming in the night. He rolls over and says, 'Don't worry, go back to sleep.' The camera pulls back and we realize he's cuddling the corpse. OK, a bit of foreshadowing, but that's fine. That's how it was in the original script. The problem was, when we shot it, I didn't like the way the corpse looked in the scene. It was a catch-22, you want your big shock in the beginning, but you also want it for the end. And I didn't want to show the corpse until the last possible second. I toyed around with it, and we played with color correction, and finally I said, 'I don't like the scene. I want it gone.' Nobody had had a problem except for me.

"This is the closest movie for me that has ever gone from idea to finished project and it comes in as close as possible to what I had in my head. They say that, as a director and writer, if you can get 30 percent of your vision onto the screen, you've done your job. With every single person's involvement on this, I feel like we've gotten 98 percent of what I wanted onto the screen. I couldn't be happier."

As of this writing, Lonnie has *Her Name Was Christa* under consideration with a number of distributors, and the producers are working to decide which would offer the best deal. It's a nice position to be in, considering how difficult the distribution game is these days. Once upon a time, there were dozens of outfits willing to gamble on a lesser-known cast in a smaller-budgeted film. Those days are long gone.

"We've had seven offers on the film," he says. "Only one of them I'm actually considering. The biggest problem these days with distributors is that, of course, there's no money up front, so if you don't want to take a shit deal, that's fine with them. There are 50 other movies sitting on their desks, made by directors who are willing to take that shit deal. Now, if we decide not to go with the distributor we like, I will probably do a limited run Blu-ray, self-distributed. Because of the people—even though there weren't a lot of people who contributed to the original Indiegogo, they need to be taken care of before anything else. And we're ready to roll on the next feature, but I don't want to start another Indiegogo before we have the first one squared away."

(If the above isn't enough to entice diehard fans of the old Tempe days, consider this: *Her Name Was Christa* brings the *Bloodletting* cycle full circle, offering cameos from longtime co-conspirators Scooter McCrae, Sasha Graham, and even J.R. Bookwalter, appearing for the first time on screen in ages!)

Once *Christa* finds a home, Edwards and company plan to keep moving forward with a new production—and another one after that—in order to stave off another decade's hiatus. Says Edwards: "Since *Christa*, I shot another short film with Kaylee Williams and Sasha Graham called *Mama's Boy*, which was written by myself and Jonathan Moody. That's going to be part of an anthology. We've shot two of the segments, *Mama's Boy* and a segment called *First Date*, with me and Shianne. And we have one more called *Skunk Weed* that Rick Jermain is going to be in. I'm on the fence on that one. I may direct it, or I may have Brad Twigg direct it."

For more information about *Her Name Was Christa*, please be sure to visit the film's official FB: **www.facebook.com/HERNAMEWASCHRISTA/**

ALL THE SECRETS OF THE LIGHT: AN INTERVIEW WITH FILMMAKER HENRIQUE COUTO

by Dr. Rhonda Baughman

I've always been so enchanted with the pull of the dark—and all its secrets and mysteries and colors. So much so that I forgot the light, with all of its hues, shades, tints and tones, can be clandestine and engaging as well. And by that I mean, I'm generally attracted to the dark in most arenas: in art and cinema, in music and literature, in men and women…but the light? I had to get a little older before I realized something very important: the light can be incredible, tantalizing and piquant, too—with a pull just as heavy as its dark, eternal comrade.

Put all I mentioned above of the dark and the light together, smoosh into a human container, add a mustache, and you have filmmaker Henrique Couto.

I also liken Couto himself to the film *Go* (1999), sans drugs of course because Couto's not into that. But the film is light and dark and music and color and character and a mannerly 'fuck you, I am what I am, and I love me and I love you, and if you don't reciprocate, well, that's cool, too, I'm over here doin' my thing.' That's honestly how I would describe Henrique in one run-on sentence.

All of the usual polite journalistic adjectives apply, too: sweet and kind, hard-working visionary and multi-talented artist, Ohio survivor and thriver, it's just that I like trying to explain his light/dark assemblage because there's just no one else like him. There's only one Couto and in the world of independent filmmaking it's important to stand out from the crowd, to be memorable, and to be a unique unit with something to say: it's the only way to survive in the industry for any real length of time.

Couto is 32 years old, from Dayton, and has two adorable pups a number of us follow on his social media. "I love Dayton. I have friends, family, and a great support system for my films to boot. It's also a very affordable area, which has allowed me to live well while figuring out filmmaking as a full-time business for me. I love the Midwest. I love the complexity of how 'simple' we supposedly are. I love how polite we are and how diverse we are. I'd love to some day film in the desert; I'm still waiting for that call to direct a new *Tremors* movie," he laughs. "And I'm a high school drop out and quite frankly I think that may have been one of the greatest decisions I've made in my life. I have zero formal education, but I did complete training to be a professional wrestling manager when I was 18," he says. So, while I took away all that information, please understand a small part of my brain thought: *so dude is not saturated in the vicious, viscous oil of student loan debt! How refreshing!*

Equally as refreshing, Couto and I share a number of inspirations and a love of animals. "As a child I was so heavily inspired by the *Terminator* movies and *A Nightmare on Elm Street*, I watched those VHS tapes until they broke. Freddy Krueger really helped me grow my imagination and learn to not be afraid of the darkness. On the other side of the spectrum I was an avid Star Trek fan; I used to wear my starfleet uniform to school. I loved everything about Star Trek. When I hit my teen years I couldn't get enough *Evil Dead*, *Dawn of the Dead* and *Texas Chainsaw Massacre*. I also became obsessed with a great film called *Eddie Presley* [directed by Jeff Burr] which lead me to finding a great deal of passion for personal stories. John Hughes also played a huge role in teaching me how powerful storytelling is," Couto says.

And continues: "I never thought I would be a much of a dog person but a year and half ago when I adopted Henwolf I was amazed at how quickly we acclimated to each other and she became an integral part of my life and a joy. I adopted Chicano 2 months ago; he is a sweet boy and very timid. He was 8 and the idea such a great dog didn't have a home pissed me off so I put my money where my mouth was and gave him a home. He's fitting in great; Henwolf only pushes him around a bit but he's slowly coming into his own. I put Henwolf in my Christmas short film, *Stirring*, and while it was fun and cute it stressed her out a bit with all the lights and noise and me not being able to console her all the time. So time will tell if I insert them into a film again,

Chicano, Henrique, and Henwolf on the set of POPCORN HORROR.

Joni Durian as Sylvia in HAUNTING INSIDE.

but I would be happy to have them pop up here and there in little spots."

Look over Couto's IMDB profile and be impressed, to say the least. I'm not sure the man ever stops working or finds sleep. Full disclosure: I worked with Henrique on a few films and I supported his *Babysitter Massacre* franchise Kickstarter, which hit its goal and then *exceeded* its goal and it was obvious a large number of folks were just excited to be a part of something genuine and artistic and fun—it's rare to find that combination anywhere in this era. But that's Henrique—making us combo happy again. "When I saw the final total I was about to walk into the Gonzoriffic Movie Show in Athens, GA with my buddy Andrew Shearer; I cried and he hugged me and we went into the cinema and I tried to watch the movies and let myself process it. It's still hard for me to understand that it happened, I am so grateful every day," he says.

Couto has worked with numerous others, including two of my favorite indie filmmakers, Eric Widing and Hoosier John Oak Dalton. "Eric and I actually worked at the same TV station; he was brand new there and I had been working there maybe a year or so. We started talking about movies, he was surprised and intrigued to find out I had just finished my 3rd feature film at the time [*Bleeding Through*] and he told me all about a feature he had been working on. My immediate words to him were "go do it, it'll be great, make it and finish it!" He took my advice and his first feature turned out pretty damn good. Not much later on he started working on my sets and eventually became my go to Assistant Director and Editor. The guy is brilliant at what he does," Henrique says and I have to agree with him.[1]

Henrique continues: "John Dalton and I had met online years and years ago on the only B-independent message boards. He had also attended a screening I held when I was 17-years-old. After years of just kind of being acquaintances he invited me to be a guest speaker at a film festival for high school kids; I went and had a great time. He had taken a bit of a self imposed break from screenwriting at the time, we got to talking and before we knew it he had written Haunted House on Sorority Row which was also the first film of mine Eric Widing edited."

Previously unbeknownst to me, Couto and I share the guest-speaking sync: I would ask Dalton to be a commencement speaker at a college I worked at in Indianapolis. It is a small world after all and collaboration is, apparently, In our blood.

"Collaboration is fascinating to me, I used to think if you didn't collaborate it was because you had such a strong grasp on how you wanted things done, now however, I find it to be the opposite. When you have a great deal of confidence and clarity about what you do and how you do it bringing others in doesn't dilute it, it intensifies it because you get to help focus all of their work through your lens."

As I suspected, the only thing Henrique hasn't collaborated with is sleep. And recently, any potential restful slumber was interrupted by an absolute asshole move by Amazon Prime—one of a few entities I wish to hurt in the pocketbook—which entailed removing great indie content without reason or explanation. Like a shitty parent, the answer was: "Just because."

"When it became clear that there would be no communication, no appeal, no explanation I was pretty heartbroken," Couto says. "Not only did it cost a me a good chunk of my general income but it displaced a lot of my work. I loved knowing my movies could be accessed easily on their platform, now many of my films aren't allowed to ever be resubmitted. I'm working tirelessly to get films like Making Out, Nothing Good Ever Happens, and A Raunchy Christmas Story back in the marketplace where folks can easily see them because these films deserve so much to be seen."

But there's good news ahead!

John Bradley Hambrick as Dallas and Henrique as Hank in DEVIL'S TRAIL.

---

1   *Pick up Grindhouse Purgatory #14 for RB's interview with Wilding.*

"Right this second I have the brand new *Haunting Inside* available to purchase for a limited time on HenFlix.com that site has every physical media release of my work I can manage to put on there. I am currently in midst of a huge production slate that includes *Babysitter Massacre 2, 3,* and *4!* And Patreon has really made an incredible difference for my work, not just financially but from a audience engagement standpoint. On Patreon you get the chance to hear about serious nuts and bolts of filmmaking. The struggle is put on display along with the celebration, and it has also opened up opportunities to begin work on new and very different types of content on top of making movies. We just started pre-production on a TV show called *Popcorn Fodder* which will be almost entirely Patreon backed; it will feature myself hosting some weird, strange, and forgotten films and celebrating them for their weirdness. The motto of the show will be 'There are no bad movies, only bad audiences.' So aside from the TV show *Popcorn Fodder* and the *Babysitter Massacre* sequels John Dalton and I are almost done cutting picture on his second feature *Scarecrow County* and I think it's turning out boss. I have a few other features in mind that I'm developing I never like to stop, I get bored and when I get bored I get into trouble!" I can relate, I tell him—the 'trouble' part, that is.

Artistic vision is important and Henrique's is clear: "I so deeply want the audience to be happy, I want them to walk out of the film feeling like they got what they paid for. I love knowing people connect with the material and it moved them. That level of movement can vary greatly, whether its a cool horror film or a stark drama about life and death, I just really want people to dig it for what it is." He's comfortable being in front of the camera and behind it, that's also clear, but I wonder what he's dying to play and if there's an dream collaboration.

"I really enjoy being in front of the camera, less so when I'm also directing because the stress can be a lot to stand up to," Henrique says. "I know I have a pretty specific look that makes me not the easiest to cast but honestly I'd love to play a character where I have to push myself emotionally. Where I have to be hurt and recover and persevere. That would appeal to me greatly. I think my favorite role thus far was as Hank in *Devil's Trail*. I loved making that film, I loved directing it and I loved working alongside my good friend John Hambrick every day on set. We got really scary out in the woods! It could be cool to crack out a film for the legendary Roger Corman but that's kind of a pipe dream. Honestly I spend so much time developing concepts and making movies I don't fantasize as much as maybe I'd like."

Before I let Henrique go, I want to know what his proudest moment to date is—there's so much to choose from and I have my hunches, but as it turns out, I'm not even close. It's nice that I can still be surprised after all these years in entertainment journalism.

"That's really hard," Henrique says. "I'm kind of notorious for not standing still long so I don't reflect as much as I'd like. I've had incredible moments where packed theaters have laughed their butts off at my work, and I've gotten heartfelt emails from people telling me my movies mad a difference for them, but I think my proudest moment thus far is a little beyond myself. When I helped John Oak Dalton direct his first feature and saw how much he enjoyed doing it that was incredible to me. It felt so great to help someone do what I love doing so much. It was so powerful to sit in the edit room and see the grin form on his face as he saw his movie nearly complete. Incredible feeling."

Check out Henrique's stuff at
https://hen.storenvy.com/

HENFLIX

Independent physical media direct from the artist

AMITYVILLE: NO ESCAPE (2016)

Directed by Henrique Couto;
Written by Ira Gansler
Starring Julia Gomez, Josh Miller, Allison Egan

Reviewed by Mike Haushalter

This found-footage film directed by Couto centers on two stories about Amityville and its famous ghost house. The first story is about a group of college students making a video documentary about what scares people, spending the night in the Amityville woods behind the famous house. The second story is a video diary of a lonely young housewife who has just moved in while her new husband is deployed overseas.

I have a few problems with this effort right from the get-go. First off, save for Julia Gomez, who plays the young housewife, I recognize most of the cast from a multitude of other Couto projects, and it just weakens the found-footage concept for me. It also bothers me a bit that the ghost seems to be the cameraman at several points. Secondly, I don't buy into the whole Amityville Horror thing to begin with, but if it were real and you bought the house, the sellers would have to tell you people were murdered there. Even if they didn't, it seems hard to believe that prospective buyers would not know of the house's infamy. Last, as a fan of Couto's work, the film is a bit of a letdown after much better films like *A Bulldog for Christmas*, *Babysitter Massacre*, *Awkward Thanksgiving*, *Calamity Jane's Revenge*, and *Making Out*.

Complaints aside, the film has a good cast, including the aforementioned Gomez; Josh Miller (*Making Out*) as George, who thought it would be a great idea to drag everyone out to the spooky woods to make a doco; Joni Durian (*Haunted House on Sorority Row*) as George's girlfriend, Sarah; Allison Egan (*Her Name Was Torment*) as George's sister, Elizabeth; and Alia Gabrielle Eckhardt (*Nothing Good Ever Happens*) as the happy vegan hippie, Lisa.

The script is pretty decent and should be of interest to both fans of ghost stories and found-footage films. The film moves pretty quickly, offers up a bit of fan service, and has a decent amount of jump scares and a bit of creepy ambiance.

The DVD release comes with an audio commentary, a spooky Christmas-themed short film and a trailer vault.

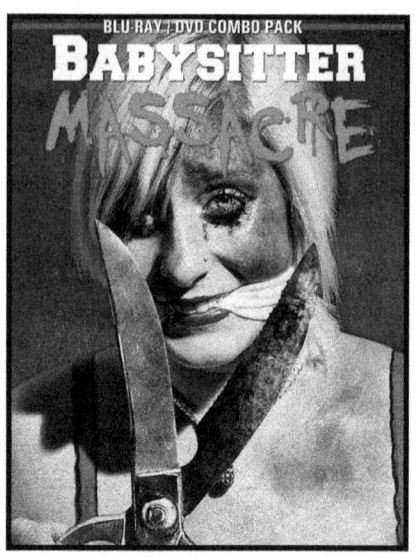

BABYSITTER MASSACRE (2013)

**Written and Directed by
Henrique Couto
Starring Erin R. Ryan,
Marylee Osborne, Joni Durian**

Reviewed by Mike Haushalter

Tragedy strikes a small suburban town in Ohio when one of the members of a neighborhood babysitter's club is abducted and murdered by a masked madman. Seven years later, still haunted by the loss of their friend, the ex-babysitters are having one last reunion before they head off to college. Unbeknownst to the girls, someone is stalking and slaying them one by one. Has the masked killer returned to finish the job, or is there something even more sinister afoot?

Babysitter Massacre is a love letter to the *Sorority House Massacre* films (particularly the second film) from director Couto. This is a smart, funny thrill ride that more than surpasses its inspiration while remaining faithful to the feel of an '80s slasher effort. Couto manages the difficult trick of updating slasher tropes to the conventions of today's horror throughout. It is a fast-paced film that moves like gangbusters, chock-full of humor, brutal gore, and gorgeous fanservice.

The film's strengths are a smart script with great dialogue, terrific photography, and a fantastic cast of lovely ladies, headlined by the powerhouse trio of Erin R. Ryan, Joni Durian, and Marylee Osborne. While they were all pretty much at the beginning of their careers when *Babysitter Massacre* was made, they all shine, and it's easy to see why they have all become popular stars in the underground film scene. They are backed by some great supporting castmates, including Geoff Burkman, Chandra McCracken, and Amy Taint (Taint in particular, as she and Erin have a scene of mother-daughter bonding that really rises above typical slasher film fare). The film also boasts very sharp-looking visuals and special makeup effects. It's proved to be quite a fan favorite since it was made, and (as of 2019) three sequels are in the works, as well as some paperback tie-ins.

CALAMITY JANE'S REVENGE (2015)

Directed by Henrique Couto; Written by John Oak Dalton Starring Erin R. Ryan, Al Snow, Julia Gomez.

Reviewed by Mike Haushalter

This is a Western that takes a different look at the death of Wild Bill Hickok and the revenge taken by Calamity Jane (Erin R. Ryan) on the men who conspired to kill him. While Jane is on the hunt, a lawman enlists the help of Jane's friend Colorado Charlie Utter (wrestler Al Snow) to track Jane and stop her before she goes too far.

Calamity Jane's Revenge is Henrique Couto's eleventh outing as a director, and it's perhaps his best film so far. This time, he has crafted an old-school Western story of redemption and revenge in the vein of early Roger Corman efforts like *Five Guns West* and *The Gunslinger*. The film has several things going for it. First is the fantastic script from John Oak Dalton (*Alone in a Ghost House*, *Scarewaves*, and *Haunted House on Sorority Row*), which tells a great story and has great characters. Next is the cast, headlined by Ryan as Jane and Snow as Charlie Utter, along with Joe Kidd as Wild Bill Hickok and newcomer Julia Gomez, whose character, Fay, brings a bit of humanity to the revenge-craving Jane. The film looks great and, thanks to some well-edited stock footage, like a much bigger production than it actually was.

It's been only recently that I have become a fan of Westerns. Over the last few years, I have jumped into the genre with both feet and am now a big fan of the films and cowboy superstars like John Wayne and Randolph Scott. As such, I was pretty

excited when I heard that Couto was working on a Western, a big switch from the genres he had been working in. After seeing it, I feel it's Couto's best work; some of his other efforts may have more of his heart and soul invested—say *Depression: The Movie*, for instance—but, for my money, this is the better film.

DEVIL'S TRAIL (2017)

Directed by Henrique Couto;
Written by Jeremy Blitz
Starring John Bradley Hambrick, Henrique Couto, Erin R. Ryan

Reviewed by Doug Waltz

Two guys with their own wilderness survival show decide to take on one of the most unforgiving terrains of all time. The Pines Barrens. Dallas (John Bradley Hambrick) and Hank (Henrique Couto) bring along the basics of survival are going to live off the land. However, this particular stretch of land boasts of being the home of the beast known as The Jersey Devil.

Soon things go south. The weather drops lower than it should for the time of year. Food is scarce. But, there are a couple of bright spots along the trail. When they happen upon a coven of naked witches performing a ritual, the lovely ladies add a little spring to their step and, hopefully, more viewers for their show. An abandoned campsite is spooky, but then it gives them some much needed food and shelter as they continue to go deeper and deeper into The Barrens.

When night comes so do unnatural noises and glimpses of things out in the woods, even one of the naked witches makes another appearance triggering their night camera. They ignore all of this and continue on to make their show safety be damned.

Probably not the brightest idea.

Devil's Trail is another in the long line of found-footage movies that started with that damned *Blair Witch* movie. I really hated that movie and have not had any love for this particular subgenre. *Devil's Trail* works because it's a super stripped down form of the sub genre. Two guys with selfie sticks and phones making a movie. Couto is the cocky one. So cocky he wasted one of his extra survival items on sunglasses. His mind is on the show and making it great. Hambrick, as Dallas, is the real gem of this film, focused on the survival aspects of the show. There's a scene where he is trying to shoot some dinner with his slingshot and is just failing miserably and you can feel the mounting frustration build with each failed shot. Watching Dallas visibly deteriorate before your eyes is what raises this movie above a majority of those other found footage things littering the cinematic landscape.

The other thing that makes the movie so good is a secret. See, it has one of those endings we really can't discuss. Giving it away would ruin any viewing for people. Just trust me in that it's worth the wait and Hambrick's performance will be more than sufficient to get you to the end of a nice, lean thriller that shows how a found-footage should be.

I thought it was way better than *Blair Witch*.

HAUNTING INSIDE (2019)

Directed by Henrique Couto;
Written by Dan Wilder
Starring Joni Durian, John Bradley Hambrick, Alia Gabrielle Eckhardt.

Reviewed by Doug Waltz

When Sylvia (Joni Durian) and Sammy (John Bradley Hambrick) lose their parents, Sylvia retreats into her own world and refuses to leave the house. She has trouble telling the difference between reality and fiction. Sammy tries to do what is best for her, but the bills are piling up and the advance he got for his new book is dwindling away fast. Add a severe case of writer's block and Sammy becomes desperate to find something to bring more money into the house. Sylvia's psychiatrist suggests board games, so Sammy goes to a local second hand shop and gets a stack of them. Soon Sylvia finds her favorite: a Ouija board.

But this is no run-of-the-mill Ouija board. At first it does nothing and she becomes more and more frustrated, until something from the other side contacts her. Soon, a group of phantoms become her best friends. There's a little girl (Alia Gabrielle Eckhardt), a punk rocker girl (Racheal Redolfi), and an Italian gangster (Joe Kidd) that teaches Sylvia how to cook, surprising her brother and his girlfriend, Rebecca (Erin R. Ryan).

At first these phantoms seem to be really helping. Sylvia is more sure of herself. She cooks dinner so Sammy can write. They rat out Sylvia's psychiatrist for being too touchy-feely during his private sessions with her.

But, you know this can't go on

forever, right?

Soon the games become darker and more deadly. The things from the board have an agenda and, for the first time in a very long time, they want to have an addition to their spooky little family. Yeah, it's Sylvia.

Director Couto gives us a nice little horror flick. Sure, there have been a lot of Ouija board horror movies. *Witchboard,* anyone? But the creatures that come from the board that make the movie. The punk rocker exudes the confidence of a long-gone era of punk rock. The Italian gangster proves that food will work its way into anyone's good graces and the little girl gives Sylvia a friend that doesn't judge her or the way she acts. The three actors playing the spooks hit all the right notes, especially Ms. Eckhardt as the little girl. She goes from sweetness and light to just demonic in a couple of beats later in the film, and proves to be the worst of the bunch. Such a creepy, well done performance. Joni Durian, as the shattered Sylvia, shows someone trying to cope with things outside of her coping mechanisms. You can see the utter confusion in her eyes as she attempts to do normal things. The normal world stopped making sense to her when her parents died. She tries, but you can see it's not working. Ms. Durian makes you embrace her confusion every minute she's on the screen.

And Hambrick as poor Sammy, the big brother that just wants to make the world safe for his little sister. His guilt over what to do with her and wondering if he is doing the right thing by keeping her with him instead of having her institutionalized is heartbreaking to watch. The constant nightmares that drive any chance of writing again shows a man on the verge of his own breakdown but can't afford to have one.

Henrique Couto has managed to surround himself with a cast that could have just made a movie about a haunted Ouija board into something more realistic. That makes it even scarier.

SCAREWAVES (2014)

Directed by Henrique Couto
Starring Erin R. Ryan, JoAnna Lloyd, Tonjia Atomic

Reviewed by Mike Haushalter

Having paid tribute to '80s slashers with his film *Babysitter Massacre*, Henrique Couto then, with *Scarewaves*, set his sights on '80s anthology efforts like *Creepshow*,

From a Whisper to a Scream, and, of course, HBO's *Tales from the Crypt*.

Scarewaves follows the final broadcast of shock jock Amos Satan (John Bradley Hambrick), who breaks the format of listener call-ins to tell his own stories of horror.

"Painting After Midnight," written by Jeremy Biltz: Joe Kidd is pretty creepy as an artist with a secret, and Erin R. Ryan is the fetching new roommate in for more than she imagined in this tale of demonic evil that is long on fanservice and short on scares. Anyone who has watched many horror anthology efforts will see the twist coming from the get-go, but it's a decent ride there.

"Fair Scare," written by John Oak Dalton: This is the story of a trio of crooks whose argument over how to share the loot from their last haul escalates to deadly consequences for all involved. Will love or family come first? I thought this was the weakest link of the film. Like the other shorts, it has a fine cast and some great dialogue, but that's about it—no thrills and no chills. It doesn't even feel complete, more like a puzzle missing a few pieces.

"Office Case," written by Ira M. Gansler: I found this one to be vaguely similar to the full-length independent feature *Last Shift* (2014). The short made great use of its location and of actor Geoff Burkman as a night security guard. It comes up short in generating any suspense or audience sympathy for Burkman's character, unfortunately. The shock ending was not quite what I expected, and I think the one in my brain was better.

"Worth the Wait" written by Henrique Couto: A love triangle sorts itself out with the expected results. Even if I hadn't known going in that this was written by Couto himself, I would have realized it pretty early, as it has his fingerprints all over it. For my money it's the best short of the four, offering a decent mix of scares and humor.

As a whole, *Scarewaves* offers up tons of nudity and a great cast doing their best with the material they are given. It looks great, better than many other low-budget efforts. I liked the framework of the radio show. John Bradley Hambrick has a great voice and makes for a great disc jockey. All that said, I think it may have been better if they cut a story and gave more time and effort to the remaining ones. All the stories in my mind could have used a bit more refining, as none of the tales was really that scary or exciting. In the end, the only thing that was killed was time.

BRITAIN'S MORAL PANIC[1]

Early in 2019, Amazon Prime made an inexplicable purge of many—*many*—independently-made horror films from their streaming service. Indie producers, like our own Henrique Couto, woke up one morning to find that more than half of their catalogue had vanished from the offerings overnight. There was no explanation, nor possibility for appeal. And Amazon refused to comment further.

So naturally, the rumors spread. Amazon was under the thumb of Hollywood, some reasoned, and Hollywood didn't like the competition. Amazon didn't want to pay indie distributors any longer (not that the pennies-per-view they were paying was breaking their bank). Then came the condemnation that there was some sort of Moral Panic in play. This argument barely held water—half of the purged films had no violence, nor nudity—but it was as good an explanation as any in light of any other evidence. And it wouldn't be the first time. I turn your attention to the UK and their moral panic over

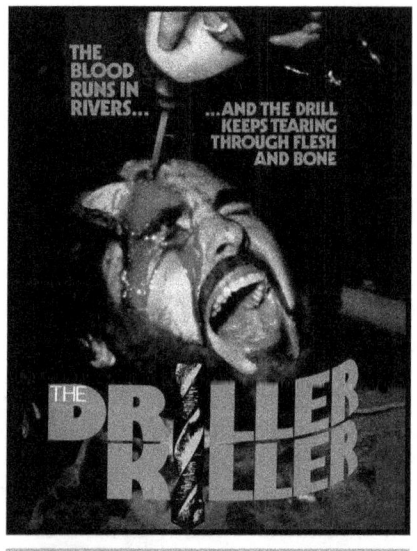

VIPCO ruins everything. Original art for the UK release of DRILLER KILLER.

"Video Nasties," beginning in the early '80s, at a time when the marketplace for home video was just starting to explode across the world.

In 1982 Vipco, the UK distributors of Abel Ferrara's 1979 sleaze classic *Driller Killer*, committed the apparently reprehensible act of advertising their new acquisition by buying full page ads in British movie magazines. To further identify their new release as *Driller Killer*, Vipco had the audacity to include in their ads the movie's box

---

[1] Portions of this article first appeared in a very different format in *Fervid Filmmaking*, published by McFarland Press.

The true monster of the Moral Panic, Ms. Mary Whitehouse. (Photo copyright unknown. All rights reserved.)

art. By these very acts of savagery, the company destroyed a large chunk of the British people's moral fabric. A large number of concerned citizens, despite few of their ranks having actually seen the movie, complained to the Advertising Standards Agency to protest the film's release and, perhaps, its very existence. All of this was spawned by the promotional artwork: a special-effects shot of the title character and one of his victims, a power drill between the two and splashes of red around. A movie called *Driller Killer* should have fluffier promotional art, apparently, for otherwise is grossly insensitive to those who may have succumbed to drill killings. In any event, it was wrong in its sheer and utter wrongness.

Add to this hysteria a nice little old woman named Mary Whitehouse, head of The National Viewers' and Listeners' Association, for whom moral outrage was tea, biscuits and oxygen. An outspoken crusader against anything not wholesome and good in the British media, she was a watchdog who vigilantly harassed the British Broadcasting Corporation and, in particular, the BBC's Director General, Sir Hugh Greene. Her "Clean Up TV" campaign made media hysteria fashionable in 1964 and Whitehouse a bit of a punching bag for satire shows.

But then another smartass distributor came along, this time with the brilliant idea of a publicity stunt. In order to promote the United Kingdom's release of *Cannibal Holocaust*, Go Video wrote an anonymous letter to Whitehouse expressing their own outrage at this film's release, nay the film's very exposure to light! Whitehouse responded as they'd hoped and decried the film, holding up the letter as proof that we'd all gone to hell and it was up to NVLA to save us all. What neither Go Video nor Vipco realized was that if you get enough busybodies riled up, someone will have to pay attention just to get them to shut up. The morality police are always the fastest to mobilize to prove that their civilization is good and decent and any outside contradictions are simply the motivations of minority freaks, sleaze-merchants, pimps, drug dealers and liberals. For who can protect us from ourselves if not others?

As for Whitehouse, like the best of censors, she'd never laid eyes on the art she was decrying. "I actually don't need to see, visually, what I know is in that film."

Thus was born the Video Recordings Act of 1984 and the rise of The Video Nasty.

Wildly open to interpretation, the Video Recordings Act rode upon the restrictions placed upon print material in The Obscene

Above: The downfall of human civilization.

Publications Act of 1959, defining obscenity as that which tend to "deprave and corrupt persons who are likely, having regard to all relevant circumstances, to read, see or hear the matter contained or embodied in it." "Sport, music, religious, and educational works" were exempt from classification. However, exemption could be forfeited "if the work depicts excessive human sexual activity or acts of force or restraint associated with such activity, mutilation or torture of humans or animals, human genital organs or urinary or excretory functions, or techniques likely to be useful in the perpetration of criminal acts or illicit activity." To wit, bondage, masturbation, sexual gratification, full-frontal nudity, bodily function, torture, horror, or anything even remotely resembling or implying such things.

For Prime Minister Margaret Thatcher, whose unpopular government was facing criticism for the handling of the Falklands War, an economic recession and vast unemployment, this was just the sort of distraction she needed. Later, she'd turn her attention towards the "scourge of homosexuality," but for now, criminalization of home video recordings was enough for her.

Under the authority of the British Board of Film Classification and their enforcer, the Director of Public Prosecutions (DDP), this Act of the Parliament of the United Kingdom declared that all commercial video recordings first be cleared by the Home Office before release to the public. The BBFC could demand cuts to be made to submitted films prior to approval of classification and could prosecute retailers, distributors and even producers if a movie was found in particular breech of the Obscene Publications Act. If works were refused classification, or refused to submit to such, were banned outright. Dozens of movies were yanked from the shelves of video stores and many were banned outright from classification, meaning that they would not be shown to anyone in the public, under any condition.

That's when police began raiding private homes. Without any rhyme or

Sir Graham Bright, proud censor. (Photo copyright unknown. All Rights Reserved.)

reason or even guidelines as to what was acceptable or not, censorship was left in the hands of the police. Officers were charged with watching hours of horror films, from start to finish, to determine what was proper for the fire. The irony that these men were not themselves turned instantly into serial killers was, however, lost on those in charge. The Moral Authority could not be questioned.

Peter Kruger, the Head Obscene Publications Squad, Scotland Yard (1981-1984), made best-of tapes for Graham Bright, showing isolated clips of the goriest bits removed from the films. He showed the tapes off to friends. "I can handle this," was the attitude. "Ordinary people cannot. I'm upper class and intellectual and in power."

Sir Graham Bright—Conservative MP 1979-1997— remains proud of his censorial work to this day. Gleefully. "They were evil," he proclaimed. And were the sources of all of England's evil, including the murder of James Bulger, a 2-year-old child abducted and murdered by two 10-year-old psychos. They blamed their act, after some coercion, on the film *Child's*

Play. A film they later admitted they had not seen.

Police were given open-ended powers to battle obscenity without definition. British Board of Film Censors to British Board of Film Classification. By abolishing a jury trial for censorship, there was no chance of acquittal or appeal.

Movies subjected to the harshest cuts or outright-banning during this early period were usually Italian- or American-made horror movies deemed too graphic in their portrayal of violence for sensible human consumption. They became known colloquially as the "Video Nasties." In modern day language, it could be called the "Helen Lovejoy 'Think of the Children' Classification." To justify the jackboots in the homes, countless studies were rigged to prove films had detrimental effects on children—always the children, though it was the adults who had their collections confiscated. Fourteen out of forty-seven kids were polled and the result found that 45% of six-year-olds had seen Nasties. And those figures stood even after it was proven that though have those kids had lied, including confessing to having seen films that didn't exist.

Non-certified movies that had been shown uncut in theaters but were forcibly yanked from video shelves and destroyed included *The Exorcist*, *Straw Dogs* and, mistaken for a pornographic film, *The Best Little Whorehouse in Texas* (from which the general populace really did need protecting). Those that fell under the 'Video Nasty' appellation included *The Texas Chain Saw Massacre*, *Last House on the Left* and *The Beyond*. In June 1983, responding to vast public outcry, finally acquesced to release the full DDP banned list of titles to the public, modified monthly as the films were successfully or unsuccessfully prosecuted. Out of the seventy-two "official" Nasties, thirty-nine were successfully witch-hunted, er, prosecuted, though some were able to get back on the Royal Good Side by making cuts and resubmitting for certification.

Now, viewed through modern eyes, some of these outright bannings were to incredibly shitty movies. For example, *Mardi Gras Massacre* (1978, directed Jack Weiss), a *Blood Feast* rip-off that's as hard to follow as it is to watch with photography shot on location in the thumb-hole of a bowling ball; *Absurd* (1981, directed by Joe D'Amato)—aka *Rosso Sangue*, *Anthropophagus 2*, *The Grim Reaper 2*, *Horrible*—which blows off its own foot with its title, describing everything from the acting to the effects and possibly the catering; or my personal favorite, *Frozen Scream* (1975, directed by Frank Roach) aka *Toxic Zombies* which seems to have been unsuccessfully cobbled together from a smut-removed sex film and an industrial video about cryogenic safety.

The hysteria following the Video Nasty list was unsurprising, given the ongoing culture clash between the Upper Class Twits and the Angry Young Men Looking Back in Anger. (When both Bonzo Dog Neil Innes and *The Damned* take shots at you, you know you've got a problem going.) David Hamilton-Grant, distributor of Lucio Fulci's *Nightmares in a Damaged Brain*, was convicted of obscenity and was sentenced to 18 months in prison. He was, however, known as "the last victim of censorship in this country." After a while, the hysteria died down.

Even today, the BBFC struggles with censorship, but with the rise of such outfits of Arrow Video finally able to distribute unedited versions of films, the marketplace has overruled the establishment.

For more information on this horrific and ludicrous panic, check out the two Severin released documentaries, *Video Nasties: Moral Panic, Censorship & Videotape* by Jake West. They're wonderful, *and* include trailers for these obvious sources of all evil.

A lot of indie guys suffered this kind of censorship. Our good friend Scooter McCrae has a tale of his own to share:

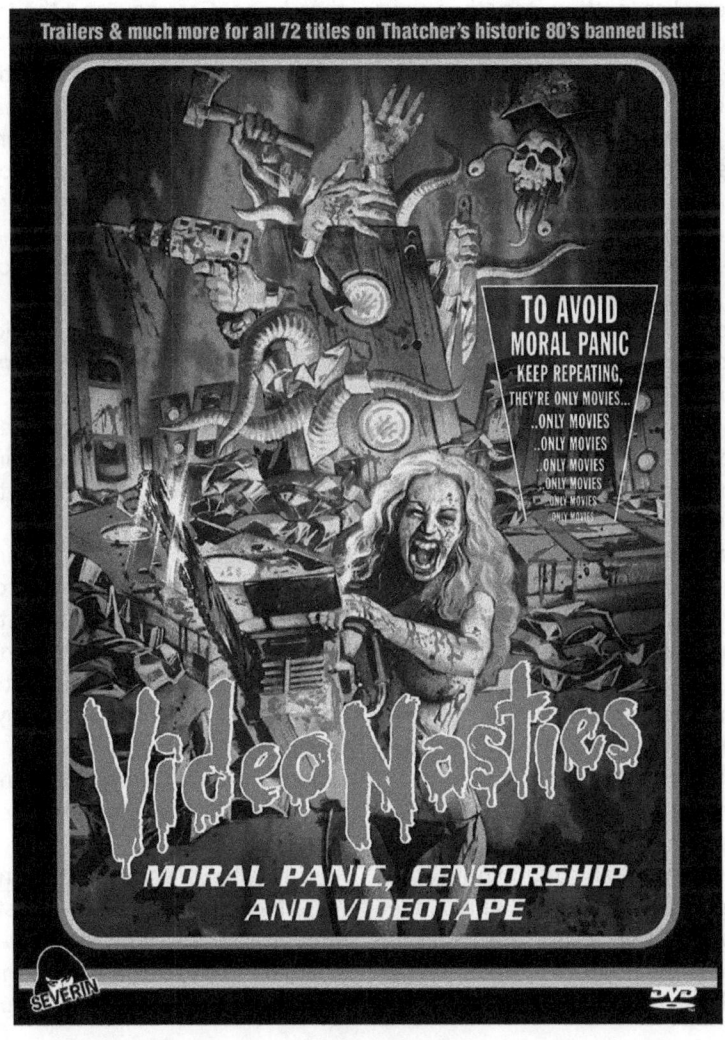

THE CENSORSHIP OF SHATTER DEAD

by Scooter McCrae

When you're a low-budget moviemaker putting together your first project, there's almost nothing more important than securing publicity and attention for your baby once it's finally completed and released into the wild. Back in 1994, when my first feature, *Shatter Dead*, was taking its first steps into the SOV (shot-on-video) marketplace, I was lucky enough to secure an article in Fangoria magazine that eventually led to it being picked-up by Tempe Video. From there, it made the rounds in all the usual suspect periodicals dedicated to these kinds of movies in the United States: *Film Threat*, *Alternative Cinema* and *Draculina* (for which I even shot an exclusive set of nude photos of lead actress Stark Raven to sweeten the deal). If you're old enough to remember all of these titles, then you'll probably also have a touch of nostalgia for that golden age of SOV movies and the support they were given in these publications.

The relative success of *Shatter Dead* within this tiny genre—along with the overall good notices it was garnering amongst the kinder reviewers—put it on the radar of overseas distributors who contacted me about releasing the title in their part of the world. I'm happy to say that Japan, Germany, and the United Kingdom all gave me the opportunity to sign a contract for legitimate availability in their region (remember, this is before the internet appeared to bootleg and disseminate titles for free to everybody an hour after they were pressed to a disc).

The only place that had censorship problems that needed to be dealt with before my movie could be legally presented in their country was the United Kingdom.

This was an interesting dilemma for me back in 1996. I do not in any way advocate censorship of anything, yet the only way my movie could now be seen on the other side of the world was for me to let go of my beloved little backyard project and allow it be neutered in the hands of uncaring strangers. I can honestly say that when I set out to make my first movie, this was not something I had signed up for or even considered as potentially happening until after the fact.

Still young enough to consider myself an artist, but also not stupid enough to think of my premiere flick as anything other than a commodity that might eventually lead to further work (well, so much for that....), I didn't make too much fuss about it being butchered in the U.K. as long as I didn't have to pay for it. Richard King, who was then in charge of releasing company Video Edge, was a lovely guy who would take care of the whole process of re-editing and submitting the cut to the BBFC, so it was no slice off my financial nose. Richard was already a pro when it came to dealing with these particular censors after a far more involved re-edit of Michael DiPaolo's feature *Transgression* removed seven minutes from its running time before it was eligible for release via his company.

As an interesting aside, when I first sat down to write this piece I was also in the process of cleaning up my apartment and happened to stumble across the initial letter I received from Mr. King on the subject of releasing *Shatter Dead* in August of 1995 (in case you think *you* save everything!). Funnily enough, I also found the *second* letter he sent to me two months later in October, as it appears I did not respond to his first missive. Is it possible back then that I knew what I'd be in for if they tried to release my movie over there? Or was I just some jackass? Hard to remember that far back, so I'll give myself the benefit of the doubt and proof of history in choosing the former over the latter. Richard also informed me in the second letter (complete with a bunch of excellent press clippings for the Screen Edge label attached) that he was capable of watching NTSC tapes, just in case that was what was holding me back from bothering to respond to him. Which, come to think of it, might have also been a valid concern on my part in not immediately responding.

(Hard to believe nowadays that we had incompatible video formats from one country to the next back-in-the-day that prevented casual viewing of overseas content, but this is one technical advance in our modern age that I heartily approve of—although the introduction of region encoding of digital media is a hateful thing.)

So I sent Richard King a VHS copy of *Shatter Dead* through the mail sometime in October. And not long after that, he received a "Notice of Seizure of Indecent and Obscene Material" from H.M. Customs and Excise Mount Pleasant Department in London—in other words, they confiscated the tape I sent him after opening up the padded envelope and *watching it* before deciding whether or not it should get passed along to the intended recipient. Can you believe that this was standard operating procedure in an English speaking country that we have an intimate relationship with in the mid-1990s on planet Earth? Because it fucking was, pally, and don't let your grandkids forget that.

Despite phone calls and a written appeal, Richard not only could not retrieve the tape from the customs office, they would not even allow him to watch it in the very same offices that they themselves had viewed the film. At this point he just wanted to see if it was at all worth pursuing a U.K. release in the first place. One of the 'friendlier' officials at the place who had deigned to even speak to him passionately assured him that it was certainly *not* worth all the effort to watch or release *Shatter Dead* on their side of the pond.

The infamous Sunday Sport.
Nothing says "You can't see this" by showing you everything you can't see.

Under normal circumstances, that would have been the end of that, but Richard pursued his contact, Loris Curci, at the Fantafestival in Italy (where Shatter Dead had played and won the award for Best Independent Film from the U.S. a few months earlier in June of 1995) and got him to send along another VHS copy of the movie. This somehow made it under the radar of government officials and safely reached its intended destination. Richard finally had a chance to watch the movie for himself, found that he liked it quite a bit, and now very much wanted it to be a part of the Screen Edge line-up. And with a couple of minor edits, the movie was released with a BBFC 18 rating certificate.

Let me take a moment to make clear what was censored and what was not in *Shatter Dead* when it was unleashed in the U.K. What was *not* objectionable: a pregnant woman getting shot in the stomach by a shotgun that blew out her unborn baby; a zombie repeatedly getting its head bashed in with a rifle stock; and a woman getting her face crushed with the butt of a handgun (amongst all sorts of other explicit gun-inflicted damage).

Here's what was considered *over-the-top objectionable*: a sex scene between two characters who were involved in a relationship in which a gun was used as a replacement penis, as the boyfriend could not achieve an erection since he was now undead. To be completely clear, the scene did involve a couple of shots of explicit (and unsimulated) vaginal penetration with a gun, although this footage was part of a series of visual dissolves to help make it a bit less 'pornographic' and a bit more 'arty.'

Needless to say, the BBFC did not find that this made the images any more artful in the least.

(By chance, I happened to end up in England a few years after all this ridiculousness had faded away, so I finally got to meet Richard in-person over a long lunch. He showed me the re-edited scene from my movie—which I was never able to watch at home since he sent me a PAL videotape and all I could play back then was NTSC stuff—and I was very pleased to see that the brief amount of snipped footage did no damage whatsoever to the original intent or the overall impact. And for that, I consider myself a very lucky person, indeed.)

At this particular juncture in video history, when the only way to see many movies by cult directors was to order VHS bootleg tapes from outlets like Video Search of Miami and Midnight Video (amongst many others), I was used to the idea that there were often multiple cuts of a single movie released in various parts of the world that might have differing footage or entirely different edits altogether due to subject matter, local ordinances, etc., so it was kind

Something Weird's release of SHATTER DEAD, released under Frank Henenlotter's collection.

of fun at first to be joining the League Of Edited Gentlemen. In some ways, I wore the distinction as a badge of honor, as I remembered the wise words of dear friend and *Shatter Dead* cinematographer Matt Howe: "picket lines equal ticket lines!" He saw this development as a bit of controversy that could help boost sales of the tape in Europe, and I was cool with that.

Admittedly, what I did not expect is that *Shatter Dead*—and its director, yours truly—would come to be denounced by name on the floor of British Parliament during the height of the Video Nasties scare. Monty Python fucking nailed it: *nobody* expects the Spanish Inquisition!

Splashed across Page 8 of the Sunday Sport in all-caps on November 10th, 1996, was just the kind of headline I could never afford to have purchased on my own: "FURY AS CENSORS PASS BLOODIEST VIDEO EVER!" Yep, that's their exclamation point at the end, not mine. These words were displayed, of course, amidst a selection of salacious stills from the movie to drive home the visceral wretchedness of it all. The lower third of this page is dedicated to explicit phone sex adverts, because that's okay and my movie is just garbage. It's a SHOCK NEWS EXCLUSIVE that begat a nearly half-page showdown of text on the vices and virtues of censorship between Tory MP Nigel Evans and Video World magazine editor Allan Bryce. Do you need me to tell you that the tape got a nice sales boost starting November 11th?

All that being said, I have no idea if it's just me having gotten older or just the general condition of the world we're living in these days, but whatever "charm" I might have felt at the time this was all happening has been supplanted by a kind of low-level dismay at the world we left behind, as opposed to the one we now openly embrace. Nowadays, it seems so quaint that postal police used to open up packages and watch the tapes we were sending to one another, compared to the modern invitation we send out to our various technologies on a daily basis to come and invade our privacy through our internet activities and cellphones, and televisions that listen to what we're saying when we think they have been turned off and rendered mute. We've invited the censors to abandon the points of entry at our countries' borders and enter our homes instead. The strangulation of our assumption of privacy has come to roost in our bedrooms, kitchens, and living rooms and we've welcomed the invasion with open arms and exposed necks. Electronic Dracula crosses the threshold and drools with delight as we crane our collective heads to one side and sigh with abandon.

YOU THE JURY

Is there too much violence on our screens?

PRIME Minister John Major this week launched a new initiative over video "nasties." Ministers condemned the decision to give 18 certificates to chilling movies like Natural Born Killers and documentaries such as Executions. They have also ordered censors to explain how they plan to cut down on video violence. But, in the week when the BLOODIEST and most HORRIFIC film yet goes on OPEN SALE in Britain we ask IS there too much violence on our screens? We've brought in two experts to give their views, but the final vote is down to YOU.

YES  says Nigel Evans, Tory MP for Ribble Valley

I WELCOME all moves from the Government to clamp down on gratuitous scenes of sex and violence on our screens and I believe there should be even more research into the link between violent movies and real-life crimes.

While I am not calling for all films to be turned into The Sound Of Music, there is a need for film-makers to take a far greater responsibility for what they produce.

I appreciate that action movies make good box-office and that producers are in the business to make money but they should be accountable for the results of their films.

I find it very disturbing that films like Shatter Dead, which feature notorious scenes like "The Shotgun Abortion" have even been made let alone given a certificate by the British Board of Film Classification.

By doing this they are basically giving the green light to violence and saying there is no link between films and copy-cat killings.

How anybody can watch films like this, where intestines fly across the room and a woman is forced to abort her living dead child through a shotgun hole in her belly is beyond me.

I do not want to be seen as dictating to people what they should or shouldn't watch but how can this sort of material be allowed to get through the net when it is so over the top and gratuitous.

I am not convinced that in today's society people can distinguish between fact and fiction.

Research

And as long as films containing violence and sex are screened there is always the chance somebody will come out of the cinema and try to recreate what they have just seen.

The truth is that there is a market for such films and as long as film-makers keep producing such movies people will always get their hands on them.

I think the BBFC should be tightened up to prevent certain films getting through and also greater research into just how close serious crimes are to scenes from films.

I appreciate that people will always get their hands on explicit or violent material through other forms of media but we should not be making it an easier for them.

The responsibility lies with film-makers who should be working closer with the BBFC to ensure we strike the right balance.

NO  says Allan Bryce, editor of Video World.

IN a society where there is a growing level of social problems, I find it amazing the Government can point the finger of blame on films and video which contain scenes of violence and sex.

They seem to think that if they dictate what we can and cannot watch on films and videos then the world will become a better place.

This is absolute rubbish and another example of the Government trying to pass the blame and make out films are responsible for the problems that exist today.

We are constantly exposed to violent scenes in the papers, on the news and in everyday life so it is foolish to say it is all down to what people see in films.

They are living in the Victorian age, if they think that by dictating what we watch, there will be less crime on our streets.

We are living in the 90s where every possible sort of material is available if you want it.

The introduction of the Internet is just one form of powerful media which makes it possible to get whatever you want.

I believe the Government is making a stance now because it wants to be seen as doing something positive which goes down well with voters.

Instead of addressing the real problems of unemployment, drugs and violent crime they are saying: "People who watch violent films like Natural Born Killers will go out and blow somebody's head off."

This is nonsense and largely the fault of the media who blame every violent crime on one film or another.

Foolish

We are all being treated like kids when we should have a right to watch what we want. Although I am not encouraging youngsters to watch porn or violence, the fact is you cannot deny an adult audience of what it wants.

I find it amazing that a handful of elderly members on the British Board of Film Classification can tell us what we watch simply on what they enjoy watching.

Young people will get access to what they want, no matter how strictly we censor films. And for every person trying to cut a film there'll be another five producing a more violent or pornographic movie.

There is no proof that violent films lead to copy-cat killings or sex films lead to violent rapes and it is foolish and disturbing to think the Government see this as the root of the problems.

LAST week we asked: Do soccer star louts deserve your cash! This is how you voted...
YES: 55   NO: 1,723

WHO'S RIGHT? REGISTER YOUR VOTE ON OUR PHONE LINES
YES: 0990 118873   NO: 0990 118874
(It costs no more than 10p to register your vote at any time)

Why worry about crime, poverty, and social justice when you can blame all of life's ills on entertainment?

THE FILMS OF SCOOTER McCRAE

SHATTER DEAD (1994). In an unexplained opening that may be fact and may be parable, the Angel of Death impregnates a mortal woman. Via this act, Death removes itself from the world. No one can die and stay dead. Months later, civilization has broken down. No one knows what to do with the overabundance of the dead. Of course, the religious have their views; so does the government. But just as explanations are elusive, there are no solutions offered.

As Susan (Stark Raven) makes her way home, she passes the dead begging on the streets. One poor man has sold his arm for medical experiments. Others are hunted down by a preacher (Robert Wells) screaming of fire and brimstone but, of course, has nothing real to offer. Harassed by both the living and the dead, Susan spends the night at a halfway house where she encounters Mary (Flora Fauna), a dead woman pretending to be alive so that she can remain beautiful forever. A "dead test"—the ability to fog a mirror—is administered often. Hidden dead are a threat.

Later, a small group of militant dead attacks the house and kills everyone inside. But soon the victims are back on their feet again. Finally Susan returns to the apartment of her boyfriend Dan (Daniel 'Smalls' Johnson). Unfortunately Dan has already given up hope…

Most filmmakers are drawn to zombie films by the trappings of the genre: the us vs. them mentality played out with violent gunplay; the breakdown of society leading to pockets of bickering survivors; the inevitable "gut munching" scenes. Not so with *Shatter Dead*. The prevailing emotion in this film is not survival but sadness. Both the living and the dead are marking time with existence society crumbling around them. The dead have no rights; the living have no refuge. Death is no release. There are no heroes and no real villains. There is just an unending march of tragedy.

Scooter McCrae, friend of *E.N.* and one of the pioneers of the SOV First Wave of the '90s, made his film debut a somber meditation on fatalism. There's little cathartic about the film and even the gross-out moments—which includes an unsimulated penetration by gun (as a stand-in for an nonfunctional dead penis), and a graphic abortion-by-shotgun that gets even worse once the viewer remembers *nothing* dies any more—are tinged with sorrow. *Shatter Dead* is nearly as bleak as movies like the anti-war film, *Come and See* (1985). It's thoughtful about the world it creates and McCrae wisely eschews any attempt at explanation. The visuals speak for themselves, as does the story.

Often *Shatter Dead* is dinged for using "untrained actors," and there are some low moments among the performances, but it hardly matters. In its short running time we spend most of it with the gaunt and haunted Susan, learning little about her but coming to realize she is the only entryway we're going to get into this awful existence.

It's grim and it's unique. And it comes with a very appropriate tagline: "God Hates You."

16 TONGUES (1999). In Scooter McCrae's mind, there is only one hope for independent film: "esthetic terrorism." Consider his movie, *Sixteen Tongues*: Sometime in the future, human beings will be created in laboratories, water comes for a price from machines boasting "92% pure!" and hotel guests have to pay to have their pornography channels turned off. Humans of this world (not too far removed from our own) live in a constant state of sensory overload, to the point of utter desensitization, and the only outlet left is violence.

With hallways plastered floor-to-ceiling with explicit pornographic posters, the Sappho Motel is a microcosm for the sewer that our technological rampaging world has become. Inside, three very lost and damaged souls are brought together via karma and circumstance. Renegade cop Adrian Torque (Crawford James), once a model officer protecting and serving, had more than 60% of his skin burned away in a terrorist attack. In a nihilistic medicinal emergency, his charred flesh and muscle was replaced with the tongue meat of the attack's other sixteen victims. Down the hall lives Ginny Chin-Chin (Jane Chase), a lab-grown assassin searching for the doctor who grafted clitorises beneath her eyelids, every blink keeping her in a state of sensual overload, keeping her from sleep and sanity. Meanwhile her lover, Alik Silens (Alice Liu[1]), rewires her own body into a living circuit so she can painfully search the "data stream" for her brother's killer. They're living in a world where the only real emotions are grief and rage. Ginny's violent tendencies can only be staved off by the blood of her victims. Alik wants to love Ginny, but is obsessed with her quest for revenge. And Torque, who was once a very good cop, now rapes and tortures suspects in order to drown out the voices of those whose deaths contributed to his skin grafts.

Except for brief forays into Torque's dungeonesque interrogation room—or when accompanying Alik's consciousness into the dizzying digital "data stream" (which feels both retro and prescient of our modern view of "cyberspace")—the viewer never leaves the griminess of the Sappho Motel. And save for brief encounters with a handful of the Motel's prostitutes, junkies, and other lost souls, the viewer spends the entire running time with Torque, Ginny, and Alik. It's their stories and situations we're required to identify with, which is rarely made easy.

Our introduction to Torque is during a violent interrogation where he orally rapes a suspect; Ginny and Alik, lovers more out of necessity than affection, meet the viewer exhausted and emotionally bludgeoned, nearly sexless despite their nudity. Gradually, their stories of abuse by the system, by circumstance, by life and by themselves, is shared with, rather than revealed to, us. In spite of Torque's and Ginny's immoral violence, our sympathies are dredged up in spite of ourselves.

As the movie progresses, the patient viewers will be rewarded even as they're robbed of the moral high ground. This is not a story that holds your hand and tells you that, in the end, everything will be okay. Like the best literary science fiction, *Sixteen Tongues* casts the future in a dark and oily shadow.

SAINT FRANKENSTEIN (2015). McCrae's first film in more than a decade is a simple character study, a meeting between two extraordinary women. To use an overused expression: "Neither is what they seem."

Prostitute Carla (Tina Krause) arrives at the motel room of Shelley (Melanie Gaydos) and listens as Shelley reveals a body full of scars and a history full of pain. She is indeed Frankenstein's monster but also Frankenstein herself, rescuing her creator and returning the "favor" he did for her. As it turns out, Carla has a story of her own, but Shelley already knows all about it.

---

1   *Punk rocker and a regular on—of all things—Sesame Street.*

The 17-minute (including credits) short film is moody and dark, thanks to cinematographer Alexander Martin and a score by Fabio Frizzi. Gaydos and Krause are at ease with each other. The unusual Gaydos, a fashion model with a genetic disorder called ectodermal dysplasia, is especially striking beneath the scar make-up (courtesy of the excellent work of Pete Gerner and Brian Spears). *Saint Frankenstein* is actually a three-person film, if you count Shelley's voice actor, Archana Rajan.

For its brief running time, *Saint Frankenstein* falls neatly into McCrae's preferred themes of study: the amorality of technology and the perversion of its benefits, that victims of a corrupt society have little say in the matter, and that appearances are always deceiving. Compare Shelley to Ginny Chin-Chin in *Sixteen Tongues*; neither asked for the "gifts" they were given. Carla's secret pertains to a corrupted society's need to dominate.

As with McCrae's features, *Saint Frankenstein* refers to a history that has built the present, showing the fallout that has already come, without offering any real hope that things will change for the better. It's a fatalistic view but not an unrealistic one. What hopes do the people of the *Shatter Dead* reality have? How do we—as a society—escape the Sappho Motel when society dictates that is where we belong? Shelley certainly has more freedom of movement than those in *Sixteen Tongues* but is likely bound by her appearance to keep to the shadows, and not by her own choosing.

It's unusual that such a short running time is as packed with more subtext than text, but that's what McCrae and producer Alex Kuciw have achieved. It can be viewed for free at **www.saintfrankenstein.com**.

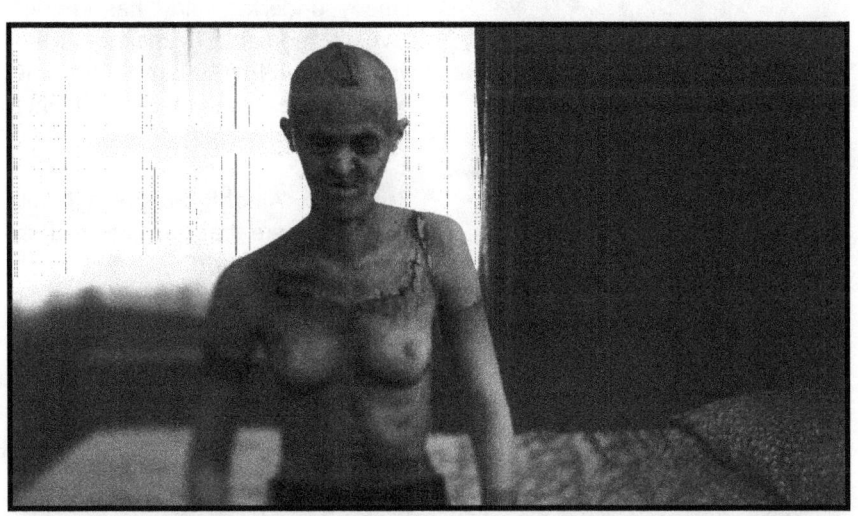

Melanie Gaydos as "Shelley" in SAINT FRANKENSTEIN.

DEVIL DOG:
THE HOUND FROM HELL
by Jason Lane

Release Date: Oct 31st, 1978
Country: USA
Language: English
Running Time: 95 min
Sound: mono
Aspect Ratio: 1.33: 1
Printed Film Format: 35 mm
Production Co.: Wizan Productions

You ever get a pet that you think is going to be sweet as anything and it turns out to be an absolute little shit? Yeah, then this movie is for you.

The made-for-TV market back in the '70s was all over the place and they made some damn good horror films. *Duel, Salem's Lot, Trilogy of Terror* (yes!), *The Night Strangler / Night Stalker, The Norliss Tapes, Bad Ronald,* and *Gargoyles* are all considered classics and they were all made for the small screen. Is *Devil Dog* worthy to be mentioned with these other films?

I dunno. Maybe *Bad Ronald*.

But while it's not great, it is good with an interesting plot, a creepy undertone and has enough "What?" moments to make you and your viewing friends happy. I, for one, would have loved to see the pitch meetings for this film.

Producer: "Alright, we got a family drama here that needs spiced up. What can we add?"
Writer 1: "Uh, give one of them a drug problem?"
Producer: "Been done."
Writer 2: "This is in the suburbs. Ghosts?"
Producer: "That Spielberg kid already had something on that."
Writer 3: "Birds?"
Producer: "Too Hitchcock."
Writer 1: "Alien invasion?"

Producer: "We ain't made out of money! Anything else?"
Writer 2: "How about a demon from hell reincarnated as a fluffy widdle puppy?"
Producer: "…"
Producer: . "Go on."

And that describes *Devil Dog: Hound From Hell* in a nutshell. Take your average white middle-class family (*wife, hubby, teenaged daughter and son*) living in an average white middle-class neighborhood, add one demon-possessed canine and voila', instant movie gold.

WHAT HAPPENED HERE?

PLOT: if you don't like spoilers, don't read this 'cause it's chock full of them. You've been warned.

Movie opens with a trio of well-dressed, sinister looking people arriving via a black, expensive car at a kennel. The leader of the group is a pretty yet stern looking woman who reminds you of the Baroness from GI Joe with both evil smile and European accent to boot. No awesome oversized circle-glasses though.

They select a beautiful German Sheppard and take it home to, of course, a Satanic Black Mass (!) complete with oversized floor pentagram, a giant evil Devil painting and black candles. Man, they went zero to sixty with getting to the Devil in this film as they call forth the dark lord to impregnate the dog (*ick*). Scene shifts to the before-mentioned average white middle-class parents, played by Richard Crenna and Yvette Mimieux, coming home from work where they find their dog ran over in

*Disney Cherubs Ike Eisenmann and Kim Richards as Bonnie and Charlie Barry.
Copyright Wizan Productions. All Rights Reserved.*

the street. Their annoying neighbor arrives immediately, describing the black expensive car that did it and how he chased it, rather than, you know, moving the deceased beloved family pet out of the street before the kids find it.

The selfsame kids are crushed due to the loss but the next day a fruit/vegetable truck comes along driven by one of the Satanists, except this time he's dressed like Farmer Brown; all happy and full of sunshine. And not only does he have some choice produce but he also has… PUPPIES. Cute fluffy ones too, around ten of them. It's an adorable scene made all the better by the ominous music playing in the background. After introducing the pup to the parents and naming him Lucky (!), the annoying neighbor drops by with his own dog, a giant Great Dane. The giant Great Dane takes one look at the adorable widdle puppy and having more sense than almost anyone else in the movie just books the hell out of there.

"That's strange," the family says.

Next up is the arrival by the family maid who, since she's wearing a crucifix, has a +8 to instantly tell evil. She works all day and then tells the dad "You know what would be cool? If you got rid of that evil dog." The father is like "Okaaaaaay. Sure. I'll think about it." The family leaves for a school gathering that evening leaving the maid alone with the adorable widdle puppy. She prays to Jesus for help and instantly catches fire, burning to death while the puppy goes to sleep is his widdle bed. Dawww! The family comes home from the play and find the maid honey-roasted in her room.

Who's a good boy? Copyright Wizan Productions. All Rights Reserved

That's strange, the family says.

Time jump a few months and the fluffly widdle puppy is now a big-ass German Sheppard. The dad mentions that he feels there's something off about the dog. His family thinks that's silly. Next up while working on the lawnmower the dog tries to PSYCHICALLY FORCE HIM TO STICK HIS HAND INTO THE ROTATING BLADES. He stops at the last minute, saving his hand in the process and watching the dog wander off.

That's real fucking strange, his expression says.

The kids show signs of being under the dark one's spell leaving subtle clues like suddenly hateful attitudes and blood on the carpet. The mom has to deal with this shit while the father is off at work late (*typical*) when she falls under the dog's control also, turning from sweet and concerned to snarky, hateful and horny. The annoying neighbor's dog ends up dead and soon after the annoying neighbor ends up dead too. The dad notices stranger things going on like his wife ignoring her

"Don't patronize me, Karl!"
Copyright Wizan Productions. All Rights Reserved.

charity work, the kids acting way too flippant over people's deaths, his wife's suddenly vicious and slutty attitude, random Satanic drawings, pentagram spaced candles, the mom and children chanting in Latin in the attic and his best friend getting killed (!) with the dog always nearby looking like "What?"

That's real mutha'fucking Goddamn strange, his expression screams.

He goes to get a checkup from his doctor and does the absolute worst thing possible by being honest with him, telling him what he thinks. Rule number one: don't ever, EVER be honest with your doctor. Anyway, the doc nods and writes a prescription for tranquilizers and suggests help (*See?*). The dad is all "Fuck this shit!" and drives the dog out to the country to shoot him. Bullets have no effect on Beezledog so he simply just leaves him there. Getting home, he finds out that the dog has pulled the ol' Droopy Dog trick where he leaves him a hundred miles away and learns that the dog has beaten him home by hours. Various other displays of demonic dog dominance occurs but, sadly, no marking of territories. The dad goes to see an expert in the occult who says "Hmmm...you've got some shit coming your way." She gives him some advice to see if the family is under Hell's spells (*they are*) and listens to her say something like this happened one time before in Ecuador, *where he hops on a plane and heads there*. On a side note, must be nice to have the money and time to just jump on a plane to another country. I can just imagine what would happen if I was involved in this scenario.

- o Mystic: "Ecuador is where they learned how to save their family from the Beast."
- o Me: "Then my family is doomed."

Getting there he's led to an old, old shaman who gives him a mark on his palm that can hurt the monster. Apparently he's just not supposed to wash his hand or do anything to smudge the painted mark which must have made the trip coming back a bitch, especially when he had to use the bathroom.

I'm just figuring.

Returning home to the US, there's a showdown later that night between him and the beast who's actually looking pretty beastly at the moment. The dog is giant-sized now with a huge Joan Jett wig, horns, green fur and glowing eyes. Not a bad looking visual as long as you totally discount the fairly bad green-screen effects transposing him over the background image. The climactic fight with the anti-Christ turns anti-climactic as instead of "giant dog attacks man" It turns Into "giant dog stands there barking while guy holds up glowing mark on his palm." The giant demon turns into fire and disappears while the dad is all "I guess I can go wash this mark shit off my hand now."

Last shot is of the family, all back to normal after getting away from the pooch of purgatory, packing the car to take a vacation. Right before the son gets in the car he looks at the dad and says:

"There were 10 puppies in that litter. I wonder what happened to the other nine?"

Here's where Richard Crenna wins the father of the year as any other dad would have been like "Will you just get in the Goddamn car, for Christ'sakes?!?" He merely smiles and drives his family away, probably planning on moving his family to a safer suburb. Perhaps in Cuesta Verde?

THE SCENE BACK THEN

1978 was a great year for cinema as classics such as: *Grease, Superman, Animal House, Halloween,* and (most importantly) *Jaws 2*.

These films cracked the top ten highest grossing films that year. Other cult classics premiered like: *The Fury, The 36th Chamber of Shaolin, Dawn of the Dead, Damien: Omen II, Attack of the Killer Tomatoes,* (the superbly creepy remake of) *Invasion of the Body Snatchers, Up in Smoke*

All of these movies premiered that year giving future generations something to watch on VHS late at night when high. One movie of note that came out that year was Disney's *Return from Witch Mountain*. Why is this film being mentioned here? More on this later. An interesting question is to wonder how this film got made to begin with. Well, the 70s were a boom year for the Devil in cinema with a smattering of Ol' Scratch's best films: *The Brotherhood of Satan, A Touch of Satan, The Exorcist, Abby, The Devil's Rain, The Omen, Exorcist II: the Heretic, Damien Omen II*

You'd think the Devil would have been happy enough for those years with Watergate but no; he's all over the place in Hollywood. And this was before he started making deals with everyone right and left (*looking at you, Michael Bay*) so he was still just a talent on the screen more than behind the scenes. That would come later when Harvey Weinstein showed up. Anyhoo, those movies usually made decent box office as the public couldn't get enough of that Lucifer. So CBS ok'd it, they made it, and they showed it…to fair ratings.

Turns out the devil can only do so much.

The cast and crew here is a fine assemblage of character actors and learned professionals that made this film a lot better than it should have been. It was directed by Gene Curtis Harrington who not only worked on movies such as *Whoever Slew Auntie Roo?*, *Queen of Blood*, *Ruby* and *Voyage to the Prehistoric Planet*, he was also considered one of the forerunners of *New Queer Cinema* (*look it up, people*). Written by Elinor and Steven Karpf who were mighty prolific but are probably most remembered for writing the made for TV movie *Gargoyles*. It was executive produced by Hal Landers and Jerome Zeitman. Landers wasn't the most prolific of producers but he did have the first two *Death Wish* films under his belt. Zeitman didn't have a ton on his resume' either but he and Landers did work together on *Damnation Alley*. The Producer was Lou Morheim, who had some nice creds as a producer on *The Magnificent Seven*, and several episodes of *the Outer Limits*, but his writing credits caught my eye as he had written the original *Ma and Pa Kettle* film AND *the Beast from 20,000 Fathoms*. YES.

The cast is listed below with their role and other films of note.

- Martine Beswick played the stern, beautiful head priestess who bought the dog. She's acted in some choice films over the years, most notably *From Russia with Love*, *Thunderball*, and *One Million Years B.C.* They have her credited in a few sources for this film as "Red headed woman" but her hair looks black as hell here (*no joke meant*). Oh well…

- R.G. Armstrong played the Satan worshipping fruit/vegetable farmer. Also puppy pusher- A superb character actor with over 180 roles to his credit, Mr. Armstrong worked in such films as *Predator*, *Children of the Corn*, *Evilspeak*, *the Beast Within*, *Where the Buffalo Roam*, *the Time Machine*, and *The Car*, but for you metalheads out there, he was the old man in Metallica's *Enter Sandman* video.

- Ike Eisenmann played Charlie Barry, son of the family and owner of an exceptional smile/sneer- also one of the twins in the *Witch Mountain* movies. He has some tremendous geek-cred as not only did who do voiceover work for *Go-Bots: Battle of the Rock Lords*, *Nausicaa of the Valley of the Wind*, and *Howl's Moving Castle*, but he was Midshipman 1st Class Peter Preston, Scotty's nephew who stayed at his post while the other trainees ran in *Star Trek II: the Wrath of Khan*.

- Kim Richards played Bonnie Barry, daughter of the family and cursed with immediate mood swings. Also the other twin in the *Witch Mountain* films. She's played in an interesting assortment of roles including *Assault on Precinct*

13, *The Car*, *Black Snake Moan*, *Sharknado 3: Oh Hell No!* and also starred on one of those horrible *Real Housewives* shows. Nicky and Paris Hilton are her nieces but we won't hold that against her here.

o Yvette Mimieux played beleaguered and bothered Betty Barry, the wife/mom of the family. Yvette had a very active acting career with highlights being *The Black Hole*, *The Time Machine*, (the not-talked-about-enough) *Jackson County Jail* and *Where the Boys Are*. She retired completely from acting in 1992.

o Richard Crenna played Mike Barry, the won't-do-anything-about-it-unless-he-has-to husband/father of the family. Another great character actor who worked on films like *Summer Rental, Body Heat, Wait Until Dark, Hot Shots! Part Deux, Leviathan,* and *The Rape of Richard Beck*, but he'll probably be fondly remembered as Col. Trautman from the first three *Rambo* movies (who was the military equivalent of Dr. Samuel Loomis from the Halloween films).

Shriek Show released the DVD in 2005 and the Blu-Ray in 2011 and they did a great job cleaning the footage as all of the copies I had seen before that honestly sucked. Damn you blurry VHS copies!! If you can, try to find the *Triple Features: Evil Animals* 3-pack DVD set release has *Devil Dog, Grizzly* and *Day of the Animals* included. Can't go wrong with that!

PERSONAL OPINION

When I was a kid, I lived for summer. Not just for the obvious (vacation, no school, no bullies, no teachers, etc.) but for another altogether different reason: I could stay up late. *The Tonight Show with Johnny Carson* was always funny, even with some humor I didn't get back then, and his guests were almost always entertaining. David Letterman may now be one of the elder statesmen of comedy but back then *Late Night with David Letterman* was just on fire with segments that were funnier than hell. But the best thing on both shows was when they had new comedians on. I saw the premieres of Sam Kinison, Drew Carey, Larry Miller, Emo Phillips, George Wallace (*the comedian, not the politician*), Norm Macdonald, man but I was in heaven, and these shows still had established acts on (Richard Pryor, Geroge Carlin, Gary Shandling, etc.) meaning that the shows that were just going to be good were now going to be great. And when the shows ended at 1:30-ish AM, I was always happy with what I had just watched. But every once in a while, these shows were re-runs. And you have to remember, back then we didn't have VCRs or DVD players to just pop in what we wanted to watch so we were pretty much left with the only options available to us.

I didn't realize until a few years ago how important the *CBS Late Movies* were to my life. My appreciation for exploitation and junk cinema was started early with my watching various creature features, action showcase theaters and the like but those Saturday afternoon showcases didn't show films like *Kiss Meets the Phantom of the Park, Kill and Kill Again* or *Monty Python and the Holy Grail* (made its network television debut here!). No, there was an entirely different breed of cinema on late at night on CBS. There were reruns on here too. *Columbo. WKRP in Cincinnati, The New Avengers*; they all had regular rotations, as did *Kolchak: The Night Stalker* (yes!). And they played some flat-out crap too, so don't think I'm romanticizing the subject. But then a gem like *the Bermuda Depths* or *Dark Night of the Scarecrow* would pop up and all was right in the world.

When I first discovered *Devil Dog: the Hound from Hell*, I think it was a theme week like "When Animals Attack" because I remember watching the very good *Day of the Animals* and the very awful *Frogs* later that week. The movie seemed decent enough introducing Satan early on and that's when I saw them.

The actors playing the son and daughter looked just like the kids from Disney's *Witch Mountain* movies. I mean, they were the spitting image of them. And there was a very good reason they looked just like them. Because they *were* them. And it was a real mindf*ck seeing them in this movie with its subject matter. I still remember watching this film back in the day…

o L'il Jason: "Hey, it's those nice kids from the *Witch Mountain* movies! They're so nice! Wait, what's Satan? The Devil? Eternal hellfire?! Oh my God…!"

Yeah, whoever cast them in this was a complete ass, as *Return to Witch Mountain* came out that very same year. Just an ASS.

I still liked the film when I first watched it. Still do. The only problem I have is that for a movie based on a monster straight from the depths of Hell, I gotta admit that I've seen worse pets, both in film and in real life. Don't get me wrong now. I know that the dog here killed several people and led other decent folk straight into the fiery maw of both temptation AND Hades but it's not like he chewed up a pair of $225 dollar Air Jordan's like some dogs I could mention. No chewing up clothes and shoes. No pissing and crapping all over the house. No barking all the damn time. Besides the murders he's pretty well trained.

You know. Besides the murders.

TV Guide Ad Copy for primetime family Satanism.

I'D BUY **THAT** FOR A DOLLAR!

by Mike Haushalter

One of my favorite activities is to look through bargain bins to find movie deals. Whether it's a forgotten A-list title, blink-and-you-missed-it indie release, or last year's hot direct-to-video title, as long as it costs $2 to $5 bucks it's bound to come home with me. But if it's less than that? Well, I'm willing to take a gamble on almost anything that's priced at a dollar and offers even a tiny bit of intrigue or interest. After all, I can't even rent most of these things for that price, and if they don't work out, I can sell them again. But when they do work out, it's magical. Here's a roundup of my latest finds, good and bad.

Romeo Must Die (2000)

The box says: "They've got the weapons. They've got the posses. And they've got no chance against former Hong Kong cop Han Sing. Gravity-warping martial arts, cool visual effects and an all-star music track combine in this revved-up action movie from producer Joel Silver (*The Matrix*) and starring Jet Li (*Lethal Weapon 4*) in his first English-language lead role. Li plays rough-and-ready Han, who shares an attraction with Trish O'Day (screen-debuting songstress Aaliyah) even though their families are rivals in a fierce Oakland turf battle. The two also share plenty of danger as they try to find the real cause of the blood feud. No gun, no posse? No problem. With Jet Li going to war as only he can, *Romeo Must Die* is alive and kicking."

Why I risked a dollar: When I saw this in the theaters I was kind of underwhelmed and never added it to my collection or even gave it a rent. Now that quite some time has passed I thought I should give it another go. And for a dollar I really didn't have much to lose.

Thoughts: I was pretty much correct in my original assessment that it's an underwhelming film. It has all the right ingredients to be a better film, but it's just a bit undercooked and under-seasoned.

Plus: Great cast including Anthony Anderson, Delroy Lindo, Isaiah Washington, Aaliyah and DMX (you may notice I didn't mention Jet Li, because he is not great in this film). Bone-breaking CGI x-rays (straight out of Sonny Chiba's the *Street Fighter* only turned up to 11).

Minus: Fight scenes are not as good as they could or should be. Very little chemistry between Jet Li and Aaliyah. Jet Li looks uncomfortable and is definitely not bringing his A game.

Shelf/Bin: Despite the fact that I am a bit of a completist this one is going in the bin.

Exit Wounds (2001)

The box says: "They should name a street or building after Detroit detective Orin Boyd (Steven Seagal). Instead, days after single-handedly throttling an army of political assassins, he's busted to white-gloved traffic cop. Someone wants Boyd out of the way, someone who should follow this advice: call for backup. Steven Seagal and DMX kick it up a notch in this searing action thriller from producer Joel Silver ('*The Matrix*') that has them joining forces in a battle against police corruption. Andrzej Bartkowiak (*Romeo Must Die*) directs, fusing star power (including Isaiah Washington, Jill Hennessy, and Tom Arnold), firepower and road-burning horsepower into scenes that push the action tachometer into the red zone."

Why I risked a dollar: When I picked up *Romeo Must Die* I thought it would be fun to watch the other films that director Andrzej Bartkowiak made around that time, including this and *Cradle 2 the Grave*, and lucky for me I found them all in one shopping trip (I think they had three copies of *Romeo Must Die*).

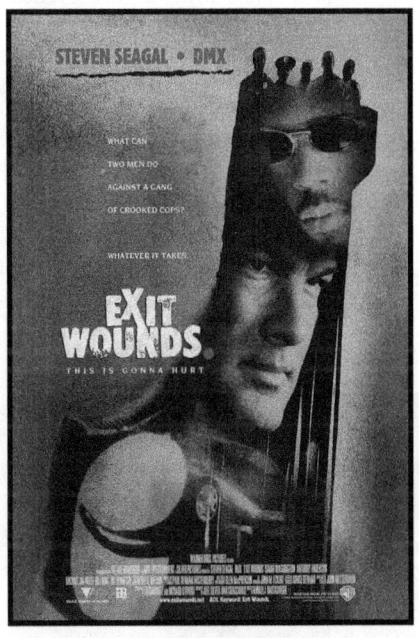

Thoughts: This is by far one of the best late-in-the-game Steven Seagal films out there. You can tell Steven was looking to make a come back when he prepared for this one. He not only trimmed down to a much more lithe figure, he also cut off his ponytail. Plus he was in a film with a lot more talent and humor than most of his previous films. Unfortunately it didn't really give Seagal the push he needed (or he wasn't smart enough to try and sign on with Andrzej Bartkowiak for another ride), as he only had one more main line theatrical release after this. DMX on the other hand made out like a bandit and was paired with Jet Li two years later in *Cradle 2 the Grave*.

Plus: Great cast including DMX, Steven Seagal, Michael Jai White, Anthony Anderson, Tom Arnold, Isaiah Washington, Bill Duke, Bruce McGill, and Eva Mendes. This is a very action packed film full of martial arts, stunts, helicopter gags, and explosions including a motorcade ambush, a brutal fight in an out of control van that explodes on the outside but not the inside, and a great one-on-one match between Seagal and Michael Jai White. There's tons of humor from Tom Arnold and Anthony Anderson, and I love their end credits bit. Perhaps Seagal's most rounded character.

Minus: Storyline is a bit iffy even for a Seagal film. The fact that one of the lead actors more than likely sexually assaulted someone from wardrobe in his trailer (he was acquitted but it's still a stain) and the death of Chrls Lamon one of the film's stuntman during the film's shoot is a bit of a blight on enjoying the film.

Shelf/Bin: I think this one made the cut and is going up on the shelf.

Cradle 2 The Grave (2003)

The box says: "The slam, the glam, the jam: *Cradle 2 The Grave* brings it! Producer Joel Silver and director Andrzej Bartkowiak, who fused martial arts with hip-hop style in *Romeo Must Die* and *Exit Wounds*, take it to the next level with *Cradle 2 the Grave*. Screen heroes Jet Li and DMX hit home and hit hard, starring as rivals-turned partners in a volatile street war ignited by kidnapping, stolen black diamonds and a sadistic crime lord (Mark Dacascos). Kelly Hu and Gabrielle Union flex beauty and strength as foes destined for a clawdown. And Anthony Anderson and Tom Arnold add comedy jams to all the excitement that's set to give-it-to-ya. No mistaking it, from start 2 finish, *Cradle* rocks."

Why I risked a dollar: Need it to finish up my Andrzej Bartkowiak binge night.

Thoughts: In my memories this was my favorite of the three, but after watching them again back to back I would put it at number two. Just enjoyed *Exit Wounds* a bit more. The action is a bit bigger and flashier here but *Exit Wounds* is more satisfying. That said DMX and Jet Li are both at the top of their game in this outing

Plus: Like the other two films this one has a cast including Jet Li, DMX, Mark Dacascos, Kelly Hu, Gabrielle Union, Anthony Anderson, and Tom Arnold. This film was a return of form for Jet Li who just looked far more sure of himself then in *Romeo Must Die*. Great fights and some cool vehicle chases. Bringing a Tank to a gunfight.

Minus: Choppy story. Sloppy Science. The fact that Anthony Anderson and Tom Arnold didn't get their own buddy cop movie after their two joint efforts with director Andrzej Bartkowiak

Shelf/Bin: Not as good as I remembered but still a keeper I would watch it again.

The Master (1992)

The box says: "Kung Fu legend Jet Li (*The One, Romeo Must Die*) steps up and takes charge in this endlessly hard hitting tale of nonstop action and revenge! In an ongoing battle for supremacy, a revered Kung Fu guru is rivaled by his American-born adversary, a disgruntled ex-student. But when this formidable foe begins terrorizing the Master's schools, the old teacher calls on Li to lead an incredible group of former students

from Hong Kong in a bid to seek retribution. Another exciting addition to the thrilling Jet Li Collection of films, Jet Li's *The Master* delivers all the unstoppable martial arts action you demand."

Why I risked a dollar: I was actively looking for this film after seeing the trailer a few months ago.

Thoughts: *The Master* is a fair Tsui Hark-helmed Jet LI kung fu flick from near the beginning of Jet's career. It's a small made-in-America film that feels a lot like a practice run for *Rumble in the Bronx*. It has plenty of martial arts madness to keep your attention but Jet just doesn't seem to have enough screen presence at this point in his career to pull this together and it is just not a very memorable movie.

Plus: Very young Jet LI kicking ass and taking names. Nice performances by the guys playing the Mexican gang bangers, and the amazing Yuen Wah and Crystal Kwok (Jackie Chan's legal assistant in *Dragons Forever*). Lots of fights.

Minus: Cheap looking. Poorly plotted and it's really hard to figure out anyone's motivation. Lackluster fight choreography. Underwhelming villain played by Jerry Trimble.

Shelf/Bin: As much I enjoy Jet Li films and feel the need to collect all of his work I feel like I can live without this one. In fact I know I can and it's on the way out the door.

Goodbye Bruce Lee: His Last Game of Death (1975)

The box says: "With the King Of Kung Fu gone forever, a Hong Kong producer recruits quick-fisted gymnast and Bruce Lee look-alike Lee Roy Lung (Bruce Li, star of *Fist of Fury*

II and *Exit the Dragon, Enter the Tiger*) to complete the masters unfinished final project in which Lee is tricked into becoming a courier for a crime syndicate. But when his fiancée is kidnapped, the gangsters challenge Lee to ascend the Tower Of Death seven levels of combat in which every floor demands a new battle with the world's fiercest fighters. *His Last Game Of Death* has begun and a furious Lee is playing for keeps!

"Lung Fei (*Master of the Flying Guillotine*) co-stars in this infamous martial arts hit also known as *Legend of Bruce Lee* and The New Game of Death from the golden age of Kung Fu cinema, now fully remastered from original vault elements."

Why I risked a dollar: I am a big fan of Bruce Li and stumbling across a widescreen print from Anchor Bay of one of his films is like finding hidden treasure, not to mention that it cost a buck.

Thoughts: Mediocre Bruce Li Bruceploitation outing with above-average fights but below average storytelling. I was impressed by Li's better than usually display of martial arts ability in this film he even looked like he was trying to hit people for a change but oh how dismal the story and villains were.

Plus: Killer soundtrack of "borrowed" prog rock samples and *Live and Let Die* Soundtrack bites. Some of the funniest martial arts battles I have seen in some time. Bruce Li shows off much better fighting skills than normal. Colorful henchman

Minus: Lackluster story, which may be giving the film too much credit, as its really hard to follow. Characterization also pretty much nonexistent. Crappy villains. Other than the previously-mentioned colorful henchman and funny fisticuffs it's over all a very unremarkable film.

Shelf/Bin: Despite its flaws this will still go straight to my Asian film collection shelves with my other Bruce Li flicks.

THE WIND AND THE LION (1975): THOUGHTS AND MUSINGS
by Bill Watt

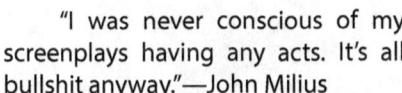

"I was never conscious of my screenplays having any acts. It's all bullshit anyway."—John Milius

Waves pound on a beach, mounted horsemen gallop through the surf, quick impressions of a sleepy town in Morocco, a boy of twelve plays on the edge of a vast chasm and suddenly hears a sound from far off that he can't quite identify, the horsemen ride through the village cutting down fruit stands and citizens alike and trampling on the French flag, the boy is admonished by his mother to come back from the edge, on the stone patio of an impressive mansion a youngish woman is conversing with an elegant gentleman in a white suit, a young girl about eight years old plays nearby, the pleasant scene is suddenly interrupted by those horsemen crashing through a decorative latticework and into a small pond in the estate's garden, firing rifles and brandishing scimitars, the gentleman rises and removing a small revolver from his coat proceeds to fire at the mounted men, rarely missing a target, until, five shots expended, the gun hammer falls on an empty chamber, "damn," he mutters just as he is cut down by a sword strike, the chaos continues as the woman and her children are seized by the bandits and the scene ends with the revelation of a turbaned individual sitting by a garden pond, calmly contemplating a flower.

Writers, I'm told, are often asked: "Where do you get your ideas?" No one has ever asked me that question. It may be because I don't have any talent for fiction, or that the subjects that interest me are not as compelling to others. It does seem to me that ideas are the easiest part of writing, ideas proliferate to an active mind, implementing same, well … A curious nature is a pre-requisite for writing, a willingness to stare off into space for extended periods of time with very little physical movement is another. A moderate facility for arranging words in a coherent form is a pleasant way to share your thoughts. But ideas, they're ubiquitous, though sometimes they have to "set a spell," while you work on something else. Because there's always a something else.

John Milius, the writer/director of *The Wind and the Lion*, read an article titled "Perdicaris Alive or Raisuli Dead," by Barbara Tuchman. The piece concerned an international incident that helped Theodore Roosevelt win the presidency in 1904. A middle

President Teddy Roosevelt (Brian Keith) makes a proclamation while appalled Natives and Secretary of State John Hay (John Huston) look on. History, folks! All photos copyright United Artists. All Rights Reserved

aged expatriate American named Ion Perdicaris and his adult son were kidnapped from their home in Morocco by a Berber brigand named: "Mulay Ahmed Mohammed El Raisuli the Magnificent, Sherif of the Riffian Berbers." Raisuli's demands for their release were money and political concessions from the Sultan of Morocco as well as calling attention to European incursions in Morocco. Because the hostages were Americans, Roosevelt said he would send American warships to force the Sultan to treat with Raisuli to attain the release of Perdicaris. He did, in fact, send the White Fleet and a company of Marines to Tangier Harbour. The situation was eventually resolved diplomatically with little loss of life and you're probably wondering what the hell this has to do with anything. Well, as I stated above, ideas come from everywhere. Barbara Tuchman, an historian, read about the incident and turned it into a fascinating article, but John Milius, a filmmaker, saw something else.

Milius turned the incident into a grand far-reaching epic, ala *Lawrence of Arabia*, using some of the same locations that David Lean did, and, it should be added, *The Wind and the Lion* is half the length of *Lawrence*, without sacrificing any of the sweep of that film. The key, I believe, to the energy of the movie is the *jump cut*. I think that this movie presents the most audacious number of *jump cuts* I've ever seen in one film. The paragraph that opens this article is the beginning of the movie and it is full of *jump cuts*. Arguably, the most famous *jump cut* occurs in *Lawrence;* in the scene where Lawrence blows out the match in Cairo and the scene jumps to the sun over the Arabian Desert.

And yet, for all the vigor of the direction, Milius constructs memorable scenes with dialogue that fleshes out the characters without ever bogging down the story. He is first a writer who cares about words and meanings of words. The shifts in perspective from Mrs. Pedecaris and the Raisuli to Roosevelt and his advisors, half a world away, (in reality, the entire film was shot in Spain, including all the American scenes), propels the fascinating story with undeniable force. A brief sampling:

Raisuli: Woman, I want you to understand this: I am not a barbarous man. I am a scholar, and a leader to my people. I am not a barbarous man. These four men have dishonored me. They have eaten from my trees, they have drunk water from my wells; they have done all of these things to me, and they have not even evoked my name to God in thankfulness. I am treated this way because I make war upon the Europeans... You see the man at the well, how he draws the water? When one bucket empties, the other fills. It is so with the world: at present, you are full of power, but you're spilling it wastefully, and Islam is lapping up the drops as they spill from your bucket.

Raisuli: [concerning the two out of four men he has recently beheaded] A barbarous man would've killed them all.

Theodore Roosevelt: The American grizzly is a symbol of the American character: strength, intelligence, ferocity. Maybe a little blind and reckless at times... but courageous beyond all doubt. And one other trait that goes with all previous.

2nd Reporter: And that, Mr. President?

Theodore Roosevelt: Loneliness. The American grizzly lives out his life alone. Indomitable, unconquered - but always alone. He has no real allies, only enemies, but none of them as great as he.

2nd Reporter: And you feel this might be an American trait?

Theodore Roosevelt: Certainly. The world will never love us. They respect us - they might even grow to fear us. But they will never love us, for we have too much audacity! And, we're a bit blind and reckless at times too.

2nd Reporter: Are you perhaps referring to the situation in Morocco and the Panama Canal.

Theodore Roosevelt: If you say so... The American grizzly embodies the spirit of America. He should be our symbol! Not that ridiculous eagle—he's nothing more than a dandified vulture.

Raisuli: This is the Rif. I am Mulay Ahmed Mohammed Raisuli the magnificent, sherif of the Riffian Berbers. I am the true defender of the faithful and the blood of the Prophet runs in me and I am but a servant of His will. You have nothing to say?

Eden: It has never been my intention to encourage braggarts.

Raisuli: Your shell is strong like a turtle's, but it is brittle.

Eden: Your tongue is clever and fast. Be careful you do not trip over it.

Raisuli: You are a great deal of trouble.

Theodore Roosevelt: [examining a rifle he has received for his birthday] You can be sure that Raisuli fellow has a rifle that fits him. Those people know the value of a good weapon. The rifle is the very soul of the Arab.

President's Aide: Raisuli's a Berber, Mr. President.

Theodore Roosevelt: It goes double for Berbers!

Raisuli: I prefer to fight the European armies, but they do not fight as men - they fight as dogs! Men prefer to fight with swords, so they can see each other's eyes! Sometimes, this is not possible. Then, they fight with rifles. The Europeans have guns that fire many times promiscuously and rend the Earth. There is no honor in this - nothing is decided from this. Therefore, I take women and children when it pleases me!

John Milius has said, in multiple interviews, that he wanted to make a movie of the Perdicaris incident for a long time after he read the original article, but he needed a hook to make it cinematic. One day it hit him that if Perdicaris were a woman it opened up a wealth of possibilities. It energized him, although he originally saw her as an older woman—he had Katherine Hepburn in mind—who is kidnapped with her grandchildren, by a much older Raisuli, and they have a crusty, confrontational romantic adventure. In order to obtain financing for the project, Milius agreed to the suggestion of making the characters younger and casting became the next challenge. Omar Sharif turned

Between the wind and the lion is the woman. For her, half the world may go to war.

down the part of the Raisuli, for which we may be eternally grateful and Faye Dunaway was unable to play Mrs. Pedacaris, due to illness. Sean Connery was cast as Raisuli, (Milius thought he was perfect for the role). Connery would star in three movies in a row that seemed to revive the kind of classic adventure movies of the 1930's. *The Wind and the Lion* and *The Man Who Would Be King*, both released in 1975, and *Robin and Marian* in 1976. All were costume dramas that were largely out of fashion in the 1970's.

Candice Bergen, (about whom Milius was not initially enthusiastic, he later admitted that she did a fine job), was selected to play Eden (not Ion) Pedicaris and that peculiar chemistry or perhaps serendipity, happened that makes great movies great. The third major role to be filled was Theodore Roosevelt, Milius' personal hero. I haven't been able to find out how Brian Keith was cast as Roosevelt, but a more perfect fit is hard to imagine. Of all the characters in the movie, Roosevelt is the person we think we know best. He was the first president who appeared on film and the first who recorded his voice. Keith imbues Roosevelt with that energy, passion and determination that we identify with T.R. Roosevelt in real life was a bombastic speaker and it would be easy to overact the part. Keith seemed to find just the right tone as he gives a grand interpretation that never slips into parody. A lot of the movie could have easily be seen as a satire on politics, war and the dangers of involvement in the affairs of other countries. The humor, and there is a good deal of it, is character driven, never strictly for laughs.

It's probably safe to say that I feel a kindred spirit in Milius as well as a shared appetite for those 1930's adventure movies, *Gunga Din, Beau Geste, The Four Feathers* and others whose own progenitors were the Victorian novels and stories of Rudyard Kipling, Robert Louis Stevenson, Jules Verne and Arthur Conan Doyle. Milius has said that he saw *The Wind and the Lion* as a Kiplingesque adventure with a *Boy's Own* sensibility. You could make a case that the entire story is seen through the eyes of William Pedicaris (Simon Harrison), the son who "plays near the edge." He could have been a classmate of Jim Hawkins or Tom Sawyer; he has that daring spirit in common with all the boy heroes of literature.

And so, a mostly forgotten, yet significant, incident in American history was deliriously brought to the screen for popcorn munching audiences to devour or dismiss according to their whims. I sat in the theatre and was totally enthralled. From the bold, heroic, opening notes of Jerry Goldsmith's glorious score to the sunset denouement of two Arab horsemen discussing world views, I was never less than awestruck by the beauty and excitement of what I was witnessing. I felt like a kid again, like I was watching a re-issue of *Gunga Din* or *The Charge of the Light Brigade* as I had in the 1950's, sitting on the edge of my seat, my feet dangling above the cinemuck encrusted floor of the Plaza theatre. It's a daunting task to pick out favorite scenes and sequences. If you've seen it and liked it (and if you didn't like it, why the hell do you go to the movies?) you have your favorites. A few of my choices:

The raid on the mansion that opens the movie. You probably shouldn't have food in your mouth when you watch it; you'll probably spit it out and that's not pretty.

Teddy's camp on the Yellowstone when he discusses the bear that they had to kill when it attacked their camp. Teddy splendidly sums up his feelings about the American character. When President Gerald Ford saw the movie he said he remembered the area where the scene was filmed because he had been a park ranger there. Milius said he didn't have the heart to tell Ford that the scene was shot near Madrid.

Raisuli talks about the years of his confinement in prison to a rapt audience of his followers and the Pedecaris family. The oldest tradition of humankind is a campfire and a storyteller with a story to tell. Connery's Raisuli is hypnotic and it is the scene where Mrs. Pedecaris, (Candice Bergen), falls in love and the children have too.

Roosevelt demonstrates to his staff and family how the bear they

Sean Connery as the Raisuli. Candice Bergen as Eden Pedecaris

shot should be posed for taxidermy and installation in the Smithsonian. Standing on his desk, growling and snarling to the delight of his children, Brian Keith's transformation to T.R. is, to my way of thinking, the centerpiece of the movie.

The assault on the Bashaw's palace by Captain Jerome (Steve Kanaly) and the Marines. I'm old enough to remember when it was okay to feel a swell of pride at a demonstration of American military discipline. I'm aware that it's a manipulative scene, but boy, is it effective.

And of course, the fabulous, dazzling, balls-to-the-wall pitched battle finale with a full cavalry charge, hand to hand fighting with between and among U.S. Marines, Germans, Arabs and the Pedecaris family, the daring rescue of the Raisuli, cannon duels, falling horses, Hollywood stunt men (four of them), getting killed over and over and over again, an inflicted dueling scar and a rifle handoff to the Raisuli leaning from a galloping horse. Even though I've compared it to other great movie escapades and as much as I love them still, *The Wind and the Lion* stands unique because of its audacity, exuberance and the sense of wonder that informs our love for movies. And there's not one damn piece of CGI in the whole marvelous mix.

Roosevelt receiving the news that the Pedecaris family has been returned, unharmed and the delivery of his bear. Teddy is visibly moved when he uncovers the stuffed grizzly bear. It stands there on a pedestal on hind legs, claws raised and teeth bared in bold defiance, looking for all the world like T.R. himself when he posed for the photographer. Teddy sits on the pedestal to read the note sent to him by the Raisuli. Roosevelt's daughter, Alice, approaches him, then turns away, knowing he needs to be alone. The short missive reads: *To Theodore Roosevelt—you are like the Wind and I like the Lion. You form the Tempest. The*

It is possible that Sean Connery has never taken anything other than a "Hero Shot."

sand stings my eyes and the Ground is parched. I roar in defiance but you do not hear. But between us there is a difference. I, like the lion, must remain in my place. While you like the wind will never know yours.—Mulay Hamid El Raisuli, Lord of the Riff, Sultan to the Berbers, Last of the Barbary Pirates.

Finally, the Raisuli and the Sherif of Wazan, in profile against the setting sun:

Sherif of Wazan: Great Raisuli, we have lost everything. All is drifting on the wind as you said. We have lost everything.

Raisuli: Sherif, is there not one thing in your life that is worth losing everything for?

Jerry Goldsmith's magisterial music swells—the second best film score ever—Elmer Bernstein's *The Magnificent Seven* is of course, the best—and you're left with the choice of watching it again right away or watching it again right away with John Milius' commentary and then watching it again.

I haven't captured in this article everything I'd like to have said about this movie; I think the subject is too rich. I can't pin down my absolute favorite in any category; books, movies, music, art, food or anything, really. There are too many variables to consider. What does "favorite" mean? What is "best of?" It's too limiting. With most things that have any meaning for each of us, it's a matter of mood more than anything that makes the decision as to what to watch, or read or eat. Unless you're an addict, that's a completely different box of crackers.

All that being said, I do base my movie choices on something that, for want of a more erudite word, I call re-watchability. There are probably fewer than a hundred movies that I watch more than once and those few I've watched many more times than that. I've compiled lists over the years of almost all of the above subjects as much as memory teasers as information requested by family members, friends and the like. I often hear the term "on so many levels." It's one of those meaningless things we say because we can't define what a thing means to us. On the rare occasions when I've used this expression I've never been challenged, but when I say it you can believe it. I think I've seen *The Wind and the Lion* perhaps twenty times and I find another level or nuance virtually every time. I think what impresses me the most is the sense of the importance of old fashioned virtues: dignity, honesty, integrity, courage, loyalty. They used to mean something. I'd like to think they still do.

SOURCES
Wikipedia
The Internet Movie Data Base
Various Articles and Interviews with John Milius
The Wind and the Lion (1975) A Novelization of the Motion Picture by John Milius
Milius: A Documentary (film)
"Perdicaris Alive or Raisuli Dead" by Barbara W. Tuchman
American Heritage Magazine, August 1959 Volume 10 Issue 5

THE PATRON SAINT OF THE UNCOOL: HOW REVEREND JEN MILLER'S ARTISTIC LEGACY KEPT NYC WEIRD

By Justin Channell

Upon first exposure to her prosthetic elf ears and legendary love for all-things troll dolls, the first thing for the uninitiated to learn about Reverend Jen Miller is that "it's not a persona— it's me."

A native of Silver Springs, Md., Miller has been a mainstay of the New York City art scene since the mid '90s, when she arrived as a sculpture student at the School of Visual Arts. Donning her trademark pair of elf ears and an art style that blends psychedelia with kitsch and a can-do DIY ethic, she's created a catalog of art that includes movies, books and paintings that often focus on her two loves: troll dolls and her pet Chihuahua, Reverend Jen Junior—or JJ for short.

Most famously, Jen was the founder and curator of the Lower East Side Troll Museum. Housed in the entryway of Jen's rent-controlled former tenement apartment on Orchard Street, the psychedelic tribute to the classic dolls brought visitors from around the world up a virtual Mount Everest of NYC stairwells to experience "the grooviest place on Earth," while also setting the scene for several films and infamous parties.

However, the site was also infamous for Jen's battles with her landlords, leading to dangerous situations not unlike the comically exaggerated portrayal of rent-controlled NYC tenant-landlord relations in MTV's cult cockroach musical *Joe's Apartment*. But instead of automatic guns, fire and melodic vermin, Jen's landlords dealt with her through gross negligence that led to a devastating steam pipe explosion and later culminated in her eviction.

Now nestled in Coney Island, the self-proclaimed "patron saint of the uncool" certainly hasn't lost any of her charm after the tragic experience and is more than willing to talk about her time creating art in the uniquely weird '90s era of NYC through the final days of gentrification.

Ordaining Reverend Jen

While Jen was searching for art supplies at Alcone, an art supply warehouse in Queens, a set of prosthetic elf ears caught the SVA student's eye as a necessary fashion accessory. She admits, "I don't actually remember why I started wearing them. I was taking a lot of acid and things like that. I saw the elf ears and

All photos copyright and courtesy The Reverend Jen Miller.

I thought, 'Oh, this reminds me of the *The Dark Crystal* and Brian Froud drawings.' So, I bought the elf ears—the same brand that I wear today, Woochie elf ears. It really is one of those things that happened naturally, organically and," she adds with the glee of a child on show-and-tell day, "I wore 'em to school. And people said 'Oh, I really like those, they really suit you,' and I thought, 'Yeah, they do suit me.'" After wearing the ears for a while, she became attached to them "like how someone would become attached to a favorite set of earrings or something." While Jen's elfin style runs all throughout her career—including live shows, the books *Live Nude Elf* and *Elf Girl*, self portraits and her public access TV show *The Adventures Electra Elf*—she assures everyone, "I don't wear them to the grocery store or anything like that."

After graduating in 1994, Jen's elf ears carried on into work in art galleries, where she found her downtime as a perfect spot to write. A friend at work recommended she read some of her work at an open mic night at a theater called Collective Unconscious.

Before her first set, Jen had been ordained as a minister through Universal Life Church "as a goof," so she signed up as "Reverend Jen," thus solidifying her nom de plume—while also building a close friendship with the open mic's host, Faceboy.

The Art Star Scene

Three weeks after the newly ordained Reverend Jen debuted at Collective Unconscious, the venue caught fire and was closed. During the closure, Faceboy moved his open mic to Surf Reality—a performance art space run by *The Toxic Avenger* star Robert Prichard. When Collective reopened "in a brothel that was closed down by the cops," the new theater needed a replacement open mic host and Jen was eager to step in to the role.

"I wanted to do an open mic because I heard about poetry slams and I thought, 'Well, that's really stupid. You can't judge somebody's art on a scale of one to ten.' So, I started the Anti-Slam at the new Collective Unconscious...and you could do anything you wanted. Comedy, dance, music, poetry, performance art—any type of performance you wanted to do."

Because the Lower East Side was, by Jen's admission, "basically uninhabitable at the time," she moved to that area and has been doing the Anti-Slam ever since—though she does lament it is currently on hiatus because she needs a break.

As the show developed, Reverend Jen began calling the participants "art stars" and used the term for her own magazine *Art Star Scene*—noting, "you know, *ASS*, so that was funny." Almost 20 years later, she'd even expand the brand into an independent film studio.

"It was this do-it-yourself idea of like, I might not have any money, I might be on the fringes of the *avant garde*, but I can still have a magazine, and a movie studio, and an open mic, and I can produce shows and movies and books and things all under the umbrella of the Art Star Scene. It grew. Other people started other

The Reverend Jen Miller with JJ - aka Reverend Jen Junior.

shows and we had so many venues where we could do stuff."

Noting that "there was no such thing as a typical night" at a Reverend Jen Anti-Slam, she admits, "I never knew what I was going to get. I kept it real straight up. Like, I didn't book acts. I wasn't trying to make my show good or make it in any way part of the entertainment industry, but over time, magazines and newspapers started noticing this burgeoning alternative scene on the Lower East Side and the comedy scene."

LES venues such as Luna Lounge were beginning to attract stand-up comedians such as Janeane Garofalo, Dave Chappelle, Wanda Sykes, and Marc Maron. "All of these amazing comedians, on like, a five dollar show," Jen remembers. "I don't know, maybe the shows were free. They were cheap or free wherever you went."

Because of the attention print media had paid to the Anti-Slam, Jen began to see these comedians show up to take part in the surprise lineups. "It became a lot of comedy," Jen remembers, "but there was also this off-kilter 65-year-old man playing his recorder or showing his leaf collection. It wasn't ageist. You didn't have to be cool to participate. You just had to participate."

Building a Troll Museum

Shortly after graduating, Jen found herself living in a room Williamsburg section of Brooklyn, but preferred to feel stable in her own place. However, her wages working at a vintage clothing store didn't leave many options for NYC real estate.

When an ad appeared for an apartment for $800 a month on Orchard Street with the note that it needed "tender loving care," Jen got a roommate and spent a week renovating the former-tenement apartment into what she described a "groovy place." Much like many NYC tenements, Jen's apartment had some very interesting layout choices—including a toilet room in the entryway and a bathtub in a closet in the kitchen. But even with the pre-existing quirkiness, the small former tenement apartment had yet to become its most famous incarnation: the "grooviest place on Earth," Reverend Jen's Lower East Side Troll Museum.

Jen's love of trolls runs deep. She can tell you the entire history of the magical wish-granting toys without batting an eye. When she began bringing her own troll collection to Anti-Slams, attendees took notice and began to bring her trolls as gifts leading to a "massive" collection of the wish-granting dolls.

At a loss of what to do with the influx of plastic and synthetic hair she had on her hands, Jen began to consider what to do with them. Her apartment had a small front room she was using as a painting studio. "People would pay money to go and look at a tenement that looks exactly like mine" at the Tenement Museum a block up the street. Jen had a thought that would change the LES art scene forever. "What if I put all my trolls up in this room and called it The Troll Museum, and had people over to look at my trolls? I sent out press releases and then I was like, 'Oh shit. I really have to do this now that I've announced this to the press.' Whoops!"

Jen continued the "tender loving care" by picking up some colorful paint and turning the apartment entryway into a colorful, inviting space where she would greet visitors from around the world interested in her collection.

After the Herculean task of walking up a seemingly endless seven flights of stairs and through the front door of The Troll Museum, Jen's brightly painted entryway was a sight to behold after the visual stimulus of the dingy stairwell. Upon arrival, Jen would give you a history lesson on trolls, and provide a tour of her entire collection—all for a mere suggested donation of $3,000. If you preferred to take a guided audio tour of the museum, that option was also available, though it wasn't Jen guiding the tour: the audio tour was a Walkman with a copy of Led Zeppelin's *Physical Graffiti* inside.

"People don't do stuff that's *that* weird in New York," Jen said. "There's a lot of weirdness, but it caught the media's attention because it's really unusual. MSNBC put it on the front page, and they didn't say it was by appointment only. They put out my address, so I came home from getting groceries and found a family of six waiting to see The Troll Museum. It got really, really crazy, but it just added to

109

the fun of the already existing Art Star Scene. Sometimes I'd have to run out and run an errand or something and I'm like, racing to get back. And the guys who worked at the leather jacket stores and stuff on the street, they just got used to telling people where The Troll Museum was."

On top of the daily visitors, Jen also began to throw parties in The Troll Museum, leading to her apartment to become a popular hangout spot for the NYC art scene. "People would just stop by. They'd be playing poker in my kitchen. It was nutty!"

From the *New School* to the Troma Team

It didn't take long for Jen to find her way in front of a camera. During one of the Anti-Slams, she was approached by a friend who was searching for an elf costume for a cable access show called *Tools of the New School*, directed by her friend, John Ennis. As luck would have it, Jen was working as a Christmas Elf at Bloomingdales and ended up becoming a cast member after meeting with John.

"I always had an interest in making movies, even though I wasn't a film major," Jen said. "Most of my pals in art school were animation majors and film majors and I liked them better than the painters. They're just more fun, more enthusiastic and nuttier than the gloomy painters."

Jen described *Tools of the New School* as "like *Jackass*, but smarter than *Jackass*. A lot of it had a political edge without hammering it home. It was a real popular cable access show, and I had characters like Doo-Doo, the Fifth Teletubby. It was a Teletubby that used to like, go to FAO Schwarz and get thrown out for like screaming that the other Teletubbies were sellouts and things like that." Another notable *New School* character was Whitney LeBlanc, NYU Hooker, where Jen would go around the famed university "pretending to be a hooker and soliciting myself because I owed $64,000 in student loans."

While *Tools of the New School* landed a development deal with Howard Stern's production company, it unfortunately stalled and Ennis left for Los Angeles. However, it did ignite a desire in Jen to put more attention to her interest in motion pictures. "I didn't know anything about underground movies at the time. I liked a lot of really goofy stuff, especially television of the '70s. But at the time, my buddy had taken me to the New York Underground Film Festival to see this movie called *Cannibal! The Musical* made by Trey Parker and Matt Stone. And I think *South Park* had maybe just come out."

Cannibal! was distributed by Troma, and company founder Lloyd Kaufman was on hand to relish in his decision to distribute the film before Parker and Stone's fame in animation. After enjoying Kaufman's on-stage readings of *Cannibal*'s rejection letters from major studios and festivals and laughing at the film, Jen wrote a personal letter to Kaufman to express her appreciation. This correspondence led to her being cast in the 1999 Troma production *Terror Firmer*.

With a self-aware story set around the chaotic—and deadly— production of Troma film, *Terror Firmer* marks a turning point in pushing the envelope for Troma. Following a successful mining of local talent during the casting of Kaufman's prior film—the punk-rock Shakespeare adaptation *Tromeo & Juliet*—the cast of *Firmer* was a regular who's who of the NYC art scene at the time, including *Tromeo* himself, Will Keenan; drag king Mo Fisher; punk rock legends The Lunachicks; Töilet Böys guitarist Sean Pierce; *The State* and future *Reno 911* star Kerri Kenney; underground punk film director Rusty Nails; socialite writer Anthony Haden-Guest; and even regional talk show host Joe Franklin for good measure.

"I think maybe I had seen *The Toxic Avenger*, but I didn't know Troma was like this big thing," Jen said. "My audition was 'do whatever you want for five minutes,' right? So, I had troll dolls in my purse and I took 'em out, and I had memorized a monologue from Bernard Shaw's *St. Joan*, and I did all the parts with the Trolls being the accusers of Joan of Arc and also me being Joan of Arc. It was intense. And then I finished my monologue and they said, 'Wow, most girls just take their tops off when we ask them to do that.' So, I got that part."

While Jen's lines in the film are sparse, her role as the script girl put her into practically every scene. Even with the chaos of a Troma movie—and *Terror Firmer* is certainly one of Kaufman's most chaotic visions to date—it's hard to miss her among the crowd of freaks that make up the fictional Troma Team. The international reach of the studio brought further international attention to Reverend Jen, and she claimed to be "bitten by the movie bug" on the set of the film

"I guess I've always been—well, like I said, all of my pals in art school were doing film. So, I've always been a part of like, underground movies and things. I was just more educated in writing, and painting, and sculpture than in movies. But I got my education in movies and TV in the best way: by doing them."

Electra Elf and Fluffer

Among the minor celebrities that made up the call sheets on the *Terror Firmer* set was Cinema of Trangression director Nick Zedd (*They Eat Scum*, *Geek Maggot Bingo*). Zedd's scene as a doctor wearing a *Bride of Frankenstein*-inspired wig while guiding The Toxic Avenger through pregnancy (remember, what I said earlier about this being a chaotic Troma movie?) hit the cutting room floor. But the

underground auteur caught Jen's eye.

"It was just this scenario, and Nick was so unusual looking that I thought 'wow' and I crushed on him right away, not even knowing his name or whatever," Jen recalled. "And weirdly, he noticed me too. There were a lot of weird people on that set, but I think we were the strangest people."

Zedd sent Jen an email asking to visit The Troll Museum, signed "yours forever," and after the official meeting, Jen invited him to be her date at a Valentine's Day party, leading to a five-year romantic and creative relationship that resulted in several short films, including an adaptation of Jen's Tolkien parody stage play *Lord of the Cockrings*.

Jen gleefully describes the plot of *Cockrings* as a computer programmer from Secaucus, N.J., who purchases the titular male enhancement device and is then transported to Middle Earth to destroy it. She especially sounds proud when noting, "Of course, there is full-frontal male nudity in the first five minutes—just to make sure it had an X rating."

She also appeared in Zedd's *I Was a Quality of Life Violation* as an old woman who gets beaten up by police—similar to what happened to a young Zedd in his most accessible Cinema of Transgression-era short, 1987's *Police State*. But Jen is most fond of their cable-access TV show, *The Adventures of Electra Elf*.

"Of all the things I've done in my life, I'm probably most proud of *Electra Elf*, because it was so ambitious. Because—as usual—we had no money to produce a show. But I knew if we had money to get on cable access—and I knew from *Tools of the New School* experience—that we could reach millions of people."

Jen and Zedd covered sign ups for Manhattan and Brooklyn's cable access stations while enlisting the help of friends to get the show on cable systems across the five NYC boroughs—a sort of no-budget syndication deal.

"I'll never forget. They make you go to a meeting before you can have a show and you have to introduce yourself to everyone. And they get to me and I'm like, 'Well, I want to have a show where I'm a crime-fighting superhero, and so is my Chihuahua, and we fly around the galaxy fighting supervillains, and I want it to look like '60s *Batman*.' And they were like, 'Well, that sounds awfully ambitious,' and I'm like, 'I know.' But I always have this belief that if you have a crazy idea, you should follow through with it."

And Jen did follow through with it, collaborating on scripts with Zedd—who also directed the series and was the one to decide that JJ's superhero name would be 'Fluffer.' The whole experience of the show truly defines the style of Reverend Jen's film output: it's like watching The Little Rascals put on a show for the town, but instead of adorable depression-era children, it's a collection of the wildest members of the NYC *avant garde*.

"People had a lot more time on their hands because the economy was pretty good in 2001, so we had tons of venues to shoot in, more people had time where could act in it and more people lived in Downtown New York because it was actually still affordable. It's not like it is now with the mass exodus where finding anyone that has free time that wants

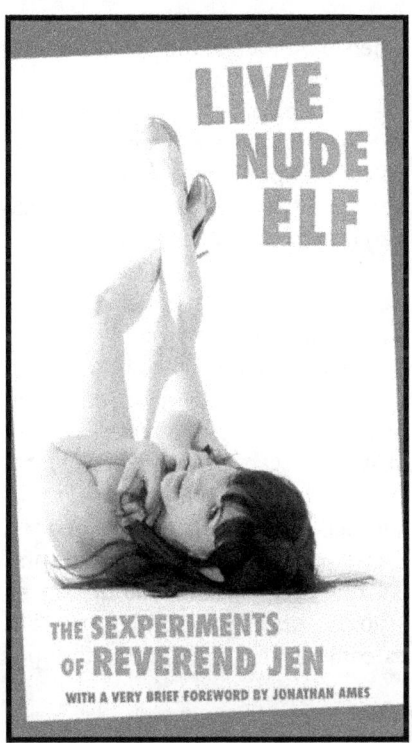

to be part of something creative is impossible."

Jen admits that she and Zedd "begged, borrowed and stole" to finish the show, including begging friends to paint their walls green and sew a Chihuahua-sized superhero outfit for JJ. However, Jen did not get the same luxury.

"I can't sew for shit, so I basically just sewed [my costume] together," Jen said. "You can kind of see how crummy my costume was, but that was kind of the beauty of *Electra Elf*. The biggest laughs of the show were when it was apparent we were immersed in total failure. Sometimes episodes would take us three months, because I was working two jobs. I worked one job basically just to buy props for the show."

A personal connection that makes *Electra Elf* such an important part of Jen's life was, after her father passed away in 2009, she learned from a cousin that it was her father's favorite show. "He never told me that, but it makes sense," Jen explained, "because he loved '60s *Batman*. And so did I— it's only the greatest show ever made."

The show ran for nearly five years, until Jen and Zedd's disintegrating romance began to creep its way onto the set. Jen admits, "We fought so much on set. We were like, throwing costumes at each other. And I realized it just wasn't making me happy anymore and it was like, I couldn't do it anymore. I couldn't put that pink leotard on anymore."

Electra Elf fans will be glad to know that Jen had written a script for a feature-length film adaptation, but unfortunately Zedd moved to his current home in Mexico before it could be filmed. However, they still speak about the potential of the project and Jen is still interested in playing the part. It'd be great to make it, but I don't see that happening for like…ten years," she said. "I'll play Electra Elf in my fifties. It'll be great!"

'Terrible human being vibe'

One project lost to the ether as Jen and Zedd's relationship ended was a feature-length screenplay about female wrestlers, inspired by their mutual love for *The Gorgeous Ladies of Wrestling*. Long before the Netflix series, this script was unfortunately never finished, but attracted attention from Asia Argento and Harvey Weinstein. Jen doesn't recall the time fondly, immediately beginning the story about Argento with a throaty, "Ah, I hate that bitch."

She continued, "Asia was trying to get like, street cred by hanging out with Nick. And she's like a vixen seductress, and *(imitating Asia's voice)* 'Oh, Nick I am very interested in your girlfriend's script she told me about.'"

Jen said was asked to write a brief outline for the film, and delivered it Argento at a club where Zedd was DJing for a strip contest—with Jen doing an "old lady strip routine where I pour little Sweet and Low packets over myself and I have this giant grey merkin." Argento arrived with Weinstein and Jen said they spoke for a while about the script, but Argento was more focused on hitting on Zedd. The final insult of that evening was when Jen found the film's outline floating in a pool of beer.

But Jen said that when Argento followed up to ask Zedd to be her date to the premiere of her directorial debut, *Scarlet Diva*, her influence begin unraveling their relationship. "I said, 'Nick, you can't be her date, because I'm your girlfriend,' but of course, he went anyway."

Zedd was later invited to Argento's hotel room, according to Jen, again under the auspice of Argento's interest in the *G.L.O.W.*-inspired screenplay. "I thought that sounds suspicious," she said. "A few weeks later, I opened Nick's journal. I swear to god, and I'm not even making this up, I'm so stupid. I guess I needed some self-esteem boost or something. I thought

it was going to be all entries about me and how awesome I am *(laughs)*. I know you shouldn't look in people's journals, but I did. I was younger, but I know better now." Jen said Zedd's journal entry recalled the event as doing cocaine with Argento, until she requested her assistant leave the room, turned out the lights and begin kissing him. While Jen said "zippers were touched," Argento did tell him that it wasn't the time or place to continue. But this—and other stories found in the journal—caused a split in the relationship.

"I threw out all of Nick's shit with a sign that said 'Move to L.A. where you belong, motherfucker,' and just stayed inside crying and chugging Budweisers. Then I called Asia and she said, *'Hello, I am in Italy,'* and I was like, 'You better stay in fucking Italy. Don't you ever come below 14th Street again or it's gonna be the shortest day of your life.' I was so angry. She'll get hers… well, I think she already has with her scandal. She's just a terrible human being. Sorry, I don't like her at all. And I got terrible human being vibe after five seconds of Harvey Weinstein being in the room."

After a trip to Maryland and countless calls from Zedd, they did get back together, "but it didn't last. It was just hard to regain trust, I guess. And the thing, I get along with Nick now, because I'm like, whatever dude. At that time, should've been like, 'They can have 'ya.' But I don't regret the time I spent with Nick, because we made some great stuff and had a lot of fun doing it. He's just not boyfriend material. And I'm not really girlfriend material, so, you know… it worked out as well as it could."

Recovering from that situation, Jen adapted her novel *June* into a screenplay, and turned her nonfiction works *Live Nude Elf* and *Elf Girl* into both screenplays and a failed Showtime pitch with *Bored to Death* creator Jonathan Ames, who was also acting as her literary agent. "He said to me, 'Don't worry about it. I had a million meetings before I scored *Bored to Death*, so it'll happen for you. It's just a matter of when and you have to keep plugging.' I mean, Jonathan's been really successful but he didn't get that overnight. He had to fly himself out to L.A. and make those meetings and not give up. I don't want to deal with publishing. I don't want to deal with L.A. I just want to paint for now and maybe do a gallery show."

ASS Studios sets the stage

After the breakup, "I was more focused on writing than anything else at the time, and also writing these like off-off-Broadway comedy musical thing called *Reverend Jen's Neighborhood*, that's like *Pee-Wee's Playhouse* but way, way more disturbing."

Held at the now-defunct Bowery Poetry Club—which was once an Anti-Slam host—the same usual repertory of Art Star collaborators would appear in Jen's plays—including the medieval-themed *The Quest for Cameltoe*, the Halloween-themed *It's the Great Pumpkin, Reverend Jen*, and a '60s-set time travel adventure about Jen's quest for undiluted LSD. "But I end up in 1666 and everyone thinks I'm a witch. It was a fun show to do."

As Jen's writing did better,

travel also took her focus away from filmmaking—including an international book tour and spending time on the road with the Tractenberg Family Slideshow Players—a family band with a catalogue of art-pop songs based on found 35mm slides.

But in 2011, Jen received a Facebook message from filmmaker Courtney Fathom Sell based on their mutual relationship with the DVD label Music Video Distributors, which handled the *Electra Elf* complete series set and Sell's film *The Hole*. Because she had her book *Elf Girl* coming out from Simon & Schuster, she was interested in collaborating on a promo video based on the TV show *That Girl*.

The project led to more short film collaborations, as well as a romance between the duo. Jen came up with the idea to put them under the name Art Star Studios—complete with an MGM-inspired studio logo painted on cardboard with a hole cut out to allow Reverend Jen Junior to fill in for Leo the Lion as the mascot. "We worked really hard and fast together making stuff," Jen said.

Between 2011 and 2012, Jen and Sell collaborated on four short films—*The Sinful Bitches, The Bitches of Bowery, Killer Unicorn*, and *Elf Workout*—all of which were later released through MVD. Lensed on an aging Sony Digital8 camera, the choice to pick such an outdated format continues the general style and tone set by the Zedd era. However, Sell's production does take on an Apple-heavy production value, which creates an anachronistic sense where the overused stock music, sounds and effects from 2012-era iMovie are thrown into an early-2000s visual style. During this time, Sell spoke often of his choice to use his secondhand Digital8 camera for its visual flair, so clearly at least some of this was intentional.

Ames stepped in to produce their first feature length outing, 2013's *Satan Hold My Hand*. The film was shot for a mere $27 budget, but still managed to attract Janeane Garofalo for a cameo appearance. Garofalo also returned for their next feature, *Werewolf Bitches from Outer Space*, but the production became troubled because, as Jen so bluntly puts it, "Courtney just dumped me, and was like, 'I don't want to work on it anymore.' He started working as a chef, and we lived together. He had invited himself to move in, basically. I'm very bitter. I was a convenient couch to crash on and a name that was sometimes recognized as a marginal celebrity. And he capitalized on that, to be frank. I wrote all the screenplays, I got all the actors. It's not like Janeane Garofalo was, like, going out of her way to be in a Courtney Fathom Sell movie. I've known her for a long time and I was like, 'Janeane, why do you keep doing my movies?' And she was like, 'The writing is hilarious.'"

Jen claims Sell broke up with her—noting that she never breaks up with anyone, "I just make myself undateable"—and requested a compromise to complete *Werewolf Bitches*. With about a quarter of the film in the can, Jen didn't want to waste what the actors had done. However, Jen says Sell became more interested in his new friends and absconded with the hard drive containing the master footage, claiming he needed the drive to edit another film.

"I don't know shit about how to use a camera," Jen said, and enlisted the help of her goddaughter, Dylan Mars Greenberg, to finish the film. Greenberg was barely in high school when the film was in production, but by the time the footage was recovered, she had already finished and distributed multiple feature films, including *Glamarus*, *Wakers* and *Dark Prism*. She directed the remaining scenes of the film—with Zedd returning to complete a few for good measure—and *Werewolf Bitches from Outer Space* finally hit video-on-demand in 2016.

"I look at Dylan and I very much see myself in Dylan, in the way I was at that age, where I had so much energy that I just made art 24 hours a day and just never slept. Which I kind of... I'm drawing right now as I'm talking to you. That amount of desire to make art is really rare, so Dylan really saved my ass."

But the negative experiences Jen has had with the film business hasn't discouraged her. In fact, she still thinks movies are the best medium for her. "I'm gonna keep making movies. I've written a few more screenplays. One I'd need a budget for. Right now I'm just focused on painting, and laying low, and on my health and stuff. But writing screenplays makes me happy. Like, sitting alone in my apartment laughing hysterically writing the

stupidest things I can come up with makes me happier than any type of art at all. What am I best at? Probably writing. My paintings are OK, but they're somewhat meaningless *(laughs)*. But I like making movies the most—even though my movies are somewhat terrible. I just like the collaborative aspect of sort of goofy fun of putting together a movie."

Circling back to the movie Jen would need a budget for, she says that she's written her first porn that "would have to take place in D.C." and describes a day visiting the nation's Capitol on the day Obamacare was signed into law. Not realizing that the city would be full of "teabaggers" protesting the new health law, the seven-year anniversary of the Iraq war, and the D.C. Marathon all culminating at once, Jen found herself in complete chaos and wanted to turn it into a movie that would be "offensive to everyone… and the best way to do that would be a triple-X movie."

Noting that the whole thing ends up in an "LSD-fueled orgy," she also believes it's "the first screenplay ever written that features a mime sex scene…between mimes miming sexual acts. It's an ambitious film."

'Pissing boiling-hot water all over the place'

Now speaking from her apartment in Sheepshead Bay near Coney Island, Jen admits that leaving her home does have some pleasant features.

"I'm far away from the Lower East Side, so I don't feel like my person is under attack all the time," she said. Jen always saw herself living in the Coney area as it's "quiet, right near the subway, but you can smell the water. You can walk to the beach."

But the pleasant vibes of the seawater only take a minute to bring up Jen's traumatic experience leaving her former home. "I can't believe I put up with the shit my landlords made me put up with. Like the hallway was always filthy, and I'd call…and they were like, 'Maybe you're the one making it disgusting.' Or 'Hey guys, the front door is broken,' and they're like, 'Well, maybe you're the one breaking it.' Oh yeah, between my three jobs I just have all the time in the world to fuck around breaking the front door every week, y'know? My landlords were so evil that—it's not like I go inspecting the boiler room and shit—but they replaced every valve on every steam pipe in the fucking building except for mine, because they wanted me out, because even though my apartment was small, it was the biggest in the building and I was rent-stabilized. Also I was very outspoken about hating them. [laughs] So they just wanted me gone and they let it rot. I mean, Reverend Jen Junior almost died in it, and I probably inhaled so much asbestos."

As it happened, a steam pipe in her apartment burst and damaged most of her belongings—including The Troll Museum—and created a deadly situation for a tiny Chihuahua like JJ. Fortunately, it seems some of her days as a fictional superhero had carried over into reality. She was returning home from work for lunch on a very cold day and noticed the heat was on in the building—"they had actually turned it on for a change." When she returned home at the end of the day, "it was about 120 degrees in my apartment. From top to bottom, the apartment was full of steam. Every cabinet had fallen off the wall from the moisture. There was water on my ceiling... about three inches of water on the ground. My paintings—paintings I'd spent months on—had bent in half from the heat and the water. But my big concern was, 'Oh my god, Reverend Jen Junior is dead. No living animal could ever survive.'

"So, I couldn't see my phone. I scream, 'Call 911' and a neighbor did and then two of my neighbors ran upstairs and people were screaming for me to get out and I'm like, 'Nuh-uh... I'm not the kind of person to leave my dog trapped in a disaster.'"

Jen and a neighbor took the risk and ran into the steam-filled apartment, with Jen herself running to the back where it was most dangerous. "I thought I might die at anytime, because shit was pissing boiling-hot water all over the place and I was getting burned and blah blah blah. And I was crying uncontrollably, I was like, 'She's dead! She's dead!'"

Jen's worst fears were conquered when the neighbor found JJ safe and sound in an unlikely place. "JJ was so smart. She hid behind the porcelain of the toilet in my bathroom, which she never went into that room, ever. Because of the cold of the toilet, and the disaster didn't break the toilet. It's the only thing that didn't break. She had the good sense to go there and she was alive, but her ears were a little singed. The firefighters showed up and my neighbors took JJ and bathed her in some cold water, while I ran back up and started grabbing anything I could. But that is how much my landlord's hated me. I know it was on purpose, because mine was the only valve rotted."

Jen's engineer boyfriend at the time assessed the boiler valve was the problem, and they investigated how much a fix would be at a local hardware store. "That valve cost $12. That's what a rent-stabilized tenant is worth. Twelve dollars. I could be dead, and we would not be having this interview. It was absolute PTSD territory, and I don't know if I've recovered. I'm a little jumpy. I'm very afraid of fires and things like that."

The battles with her landlords continued until August 2016, when she was finally evicted from the space. As soon as she had vacated the space, it was quickly renovated into an expensive apartment—so expensive that Jen claims no one has moved in since. "No one lives in that building anymore. It's basically like the whole block is being destroyed. It's really depressing. The first few times I would go back to that block, I would start crying. I had to numb myself to it."

But Jen is still positive that Troll Museum will come back in some form—noting that she would love to run a Troll Museum bar "if I hit Mega Millions...even though I don't drink anymore. It would be like a theater."

Here's hoping that someday, Jen can bring the grooviest place on Earth back to NYC.

www.ingramcontent.com/pod-product-compliance
Lightning Source LLC
Chambersburg PA
CBHW071309060426
42444CB00034B/1747